Excel

YEAR 8

English Workbook

ESSENTIAL skills

Get the Results You Want!

PASCAL PRESS

Jane Baker

Reprinted 2001, 2002, 2003, 2004, 2005, 2006, 2008, 2009, 2010, 2011

Updated in 2012 for the Australian Curriculum

Reprinted 2013, 2014, 2016, 2017, 2019, 2021 (twice), 2022, 2023, 2024

ISBN 978 1 74020 037 0

Pascal Press
PO Box 250
Glebe NSW 2037
(02) 9198 1748
www.pascalpress.com.au

Publisher: Vivienne Joannou
Project editor: Mark Dixon
Edited by Valerie Marlborough and Frances Wade
Typeset by The Type Group and Grizzly Graphics (Leanne Richters)
Cover by DiZign Pty Ltd
Printed by Vivar Printing/Green Giant Press

CONTENTS

Index of punctuation and grammar content

Chapter	Punctuation	Grammar
1 Speech	Capitals and full stops	The simple sentence (subject and predicate)
2 Short story	Paragraphs	Compound sentences and relative clauses
3 Newspaper report	Apostrophes of possession	Subject–verb agreement
4 Advertisement	Full stops, question and exclamation marks	Relative pronouns: who, whom, whose, which, that
5 Script	Dialogue (paragraphing and inverted commas)	Verbs (infinitives and finite verbs)
6 Cartoon	Commas (separating list items and activities; separating words and definitions)	Finite verbs (present participles and auxiliaries)
7 Poem	Colons (before a quotation; introducing a list or explanation)	Finite verbs (past participles and auxiliaries)
8 Explanation/ Instruction	Dashes and hyphens	Avoiding floating participles
9 Exposition	Apostrophe of contraction	Verb forms that act like adjectives
10 Interview	Brackets and dashes	Prepositions
11 Music review	Direct speech and inverted commas	Prepositions for special situations
12 Radio advertisement	Revision (apostrophes of possession and abbreviation)	Personal pronouns
13 Magazine article	Revision (inverted commas)	Nouns (common, proper and abstract)
14 Classified advertisement	General revision	The verb *to be*
15 Factual description	General revision	General revision

To the student

This book is designed to help you master the basic skills of writing and understanding English. It will help you follow work you are doing in class by providing clear text commentaries on all the different kinds of writing you are required to do at school.

The work in each chapter develops in stages from chapter 1 to chapter 15. As you work through the chapters you will find you are managing harder work without difficulty.

To use this book you will need the assistance of a good dictionary. A Macquarie, an Oxford or a Collins dictionary will be the most helpful.

Carefully examine the examples at the beginning of each exercise before you begin writing. These will show you how to do the exercise. Learn any rules that apply to the exercises so that you can use them when you write in class.

Read the questions carefully before writing so that you answer exactly what is asked. In multiple-choice questions choose the most accurate answer. Some may be possible answers, but there will always be one that is the best answer.

When you approach the writing tasks at the end of each chapter try to use what you have learned in that chapter to help you write a good paragraph or whole text.

Your use of this book means you want to improve your writing skills. If you use it carefully, your writing will certainly improve.

Good luck!

Jane Baker

CHAPTER 1

Speech

STRUCTURE

introduction, including:
- *greeting*
- *opening remarks about subject of speech*

body of speech:
- *examples of the issue*
- *direct approach to audience about issue*

conclusion:
- *restates issue*
- *offers solution*

From an Address to the Constitutional Convention 1998

As a Jagera elder from Queensland, I pay respect to the elders of this tribal country. Fellow Australians, I speak to you today with a heavy heart …

You came to my country. You invaded my land. You took our earth (our everything). You poisoned my waterholes. You gave away my land. You imposed your law on my people. You ignored the instructions of liberal colonial secretaries to deal with us and respect us.

And then, 150 years ago, you were given self-government. You established your own parliaments and your own governments. And a century ago you agreed among yourselves to establish your federation. And then, slowly, you began to change. You began to do what the British had told you to do before self-government. You began to accept my people had rights: that they were entitled to respect, that we were God's children too.

You employed us, paying us, on some occasions, a fair wage. You allowed us to serve in your army, to serve and honour your King and your country. You even elected me to your parliament. And today you have a growing articulate, educated body of indigenous people who more and more control their own future, a people who will play an increasing role in this country. They are a people who already bring honour to the country in sports, the arts and intellectual activities.

Mr Chairman, fellow delegates, you did not ask my people if you could come here. You did not ask my people if you could occupy our land. You did not ask my people if you could stop us from living our traditional lives. You did not ask my people if we would wish to live under your laws, under your government and in your federation …

As I said, I have a heavy heart. I ask you: what are you doing? Are you not already divided enough on other issues, real issues, real problems? Why are you diverting attention from these issues? …

From the bottom of my heart, I pray you: stop this senseless division. Let us work together on the real issues. Let us solve those problems which haunt my people—the problems of land. Of health, of unemployment, of the despair and hopelessness which leads even to suicide. Let us unite this country, not divide it ever.

Neville Bonner, first Aboriginal Senator in the Federal Parliament of Australia
Report of the Constitutional Convention, Vol. 3, pp. 261–263,
Commonwealth of Australia, 1998

LANGUAGE FEATURES

direct personal inclusion of audience

very short parallel sentences are effective factual accusations

direct accusation in use of personal pronouns 'you'/'your'

repetition of same sentence structure—has cumulative effect of wrong piled on wrong

simple statements, with no conditions, emphasise this is fact

repetition of opening phrase ties ideas together, jogs audience's memory

questions demand audience response

personal appeal directly to audience make it their responsibility

'Let us' is an inclusive term—does not blame anyone—invites cooperation

Comprehension

1 Insert the missing word. Neville Bonner was a member of the ____________________ people.

2 Senator Bonner speaks *with a heavy heart*. This means he:

a is sad and worried **b** is suffering from a heart condition **c** has no hope

3 Underline the correct answer. The convention was held in Canberra. To whom did Mr Bonner pay his respects in his opening remarks?

a the chairman of the convention
b the elders of the Canberra region's First Nations people
c the prime minister and cabinet
d the delegates at the convention

4 Underline the correct answer. The *you* to whom Mr Bonner refers are:

a convention delegates
b the government of Australians
c all Australians
d non-Indigenous Australians

5 Name two examples Senator Bonner gives of the ways in which First Nations people have brought honour to Australia.

a ____________________

b ____________________

6 Early European settlers acted in accordance with the instructions given them by British officials. Is this true or false? ____________________

7 European dealings with First Nations people in Australia after 1850 were always just. Is this true or false?

____

8 What did Senator Bonner ask the members of the convention to do?

a ____________________

b ____________________

Writing skills

1 Underline the correct answer. Neville Bonner's first sentence is:

a a statement **b** a greeting **c** an introduction and a greeting

2 In two lines this first sentence tells us from what point of view he is speaking. Is this true or false?

____

3 The repetition of a single word throughout the speech makes it appeal directly to each listener. What is that word? ____________________

4 Underline the correct answer. Paragraph 2 is written in short sentences to:

a emphasise fact
b be brief
c be heard as an accusation
d emphasise how total was the loss suffered by the Aborigines

5 This speech contains very few adjectives. What kind of word has Mr Bonner used to carry the weight of his argument? (See paragraph 2.) ____________________

6 What modifying phrase tells us that not all Aborigines were paid a fair wage? ____________________.

7 Underline two correct answers. Paragraph 7 marks:

a a change of subject
b a change of tone
c a new aspect of the subject of the speech
d a new engagement with the audience

8 Complete the last word. The appeal that follows in paragraph 7 changes the tone of the speech from one of accusation to one of co____________________.

9 Which word repeated emphasises this new tone? ____________________

10 Underline the correct answer. The phrase *heavy heart* underlines the overall mood of the speech. This mood is one of:

a anger **b** sorrow **c** resentment **d** guilt

11 The pronouns *I*, *we*, *us* and *you* often occur in speeches. In Senator Bonner's speech, the use of the pronouns *I* and *you* is intentional because they:

a are inclusive (inviting listeners to become involved in the issues)

b personalise the issues (so people will listen instead of hear and forget)

c offend people **d** are direct

Tick three correct statements and cross with an ✗ the incorrect one.

> A famous man once said of his speechmaking:
> *First I tell them what I'm going to tell them.*
> *Then I tell them.*
> *Then I tell them what I told them.*
> This is a clever summation of the successful speaker's technique.

Vocabulary

appeal	**homily**	**address**	**dissertation**	**indictment**
proclamation	**oration**	**eulogy**	**sermon**	**lecture**

All these words are to do with speaking in public. All speeches have their own purpose and their own style. Senator Bonner's speech is both an **address** and an **appeal**. Learn the meaning of each word and then learn to spell it using the Look, Cover, Write and Check method.

Look: Study the word closely, paying special attention to the difficult parts (e.g. silent letters).
Cover: Cover the word and try to see it in your mind's eye.
Write: Write the word without looking back.
Check: Check your spelling. If it is not correct, repeat the process.

Focus on punctuation

Capitals and full stops

- **Capital letters** are used to begin sentences, for the names of people and countries, and for titles.
- **Full stops** end sentences and mark the point of abbreviation in most words except really common abbreviations like *VC, CEO.*
  e.g. *The first Australian to be awarded a VC was Capt. NR Howse in July 1900 in South Africa.*
- Abbreviations like *Mr, Ms* and *Dr* do not end in full stops in modern English writing.

1 Insert all missing full stops.

a Rev John Flynn **b** The Rt Hon Justice Tonelli **c** Flt Lt Ellen Marcos

2 Insert all missing capital letters

a anzac day 25 april ____________________ **b** hmas Melbourne ____________________

c cathy freeman ____________________ **d** sydney olympic games ____________________

e e.k. golding and sons, jewellers ____________________

f emperor napoleon of france invaded Russia. ____________________

____

3 Insert all missing full stops and capital letters.

- **a** the cosmopolitan city of sarajevo was tragically devastated during the bosnian war
- **b** uruguayans drink a thick tea called maté made from the leaves of the ilex shrub
- **c** paul keating's speech known as the redfern park statement was the first official public admission that first australians had suffered at the hands of european settlers

4 Insert all missing capitals and full stops.

The australian arts scene has seen significant contributions by first nations writers, singers, actors, poets, dancers and song writers—david gulpilil, ernie dingo, maroochy baramba, jimmy chi, mudrooroo, oodgeroo noonuccal, possum tjapaltjari and leah purcell, not to mention the bangarra dance theatre, to name but a few

Select a word

Make verbs of these nouns.

1 proclamation ________________	**2** eulogy ________________
3 indictment ________________	**4** appeal ________________
5 oration ________________	**6** eulogy ________________

Grammar

Sentence

A **simple sentence** has a **predicate** containing a verb and a subject which does whatever is in the predicate, e.g.

John hit Bill. (*John hit Bill.*)
Subject Predicate Subject Verb

1 Underline the subject and the predicate in the following.

- **a** Nova Peris-Kneebone was one of our Olympic athletes in the Nineties.
- **b** The first Australian cricket internationals were an all-Aboriginal team.
- **c** The Australian Women's Netball team is the reigning world champion.
- **d** Our high school plays touch football.

2 Write S beside the following if they are sentences, X if they are not.

___ **a** Going to the beach tomorrow.

___ **b** Frying pans on a barbecue in the sunshine.

___ **c** Dad enjoys grilling prawns on the barbecue.

___ **d** Under the shade of the tree the children played chess.

3 Underline the predicate in these sentences.

- **a** Rock fishing is a dangerous pastime.
- **b** Climbing in the Himalayas has become a popular activity.
- **c** Speleologists or cave explorers see wonderful subterranean chambers.
- **d** Bacteriologists find their pleasure in invisible worlds under the microscope.

4 These sentences are missing their subjects. Write the appropriate subject in each gap to complete the sentences.

our friends lizards gaily striped fish the bushwalkers lightning

a ____________________ were lost in the Blue Mountains for three days.

b In a storm ______________ strikes the highest point from the ground.

c ________________________ inhabit the Great Barrier Reef.

d Under thorny bushes _________________ sleep safely away from predators.

e _______________________ run three thousand sheep on their property in a good season.

Word study

1 Where would these speeches be delivered?

a sermon in a ______________________ **b** indictment in a ______________________

c lecture in a ______________________ **d** eulogy at a ______________________

2 Match each speech to the person who would give it.

a king or his herald a professor a minister of religion a prosecutor

a homily _______________ **b** proclamation ____________________

c indictment _______________ **d** dissertation ____________________

3 Insert a word from the vocabulary list in the following.

a The referee dismissed Paul's ______________________ against being 'sin-binned'.

b 'Clean your shoes every day. No well-groomed person wears dirty shoes.' This was my mother's favourite ______________________

c Year 8 attended a ______________________ on marsupials at the CSIRO.

d Our school captain's farewell ________________________ on student democracy received a standing ovation.

4 Replace the underlined speech words with a more appropriate word.

a Harry's <u>funeral lecture</u> for his drowned friend comforted the family. ______________________

b The minister's <u>proclamation</u> about caring for your neighbour was heard attentively. _________________

c Professor Hyles's <u>lengthy address</u> on the molecular structure of the mutating influenza virus was boring. ______________________

d The disaster relief <u>address</u> raised thousands of dollars. ______________________

e Mrs Bird's <u>oration</u> to the garden club was full of funny anecdotes. ______________________

Evaluating other people's writing

Whoever heard of a racist penguin? I have never heard a fairy penguin announce at the top of its voice, 'Don't trust them dirty, rotten emperor penguins. Feed kids toenails they do.'

Sounds quite mad, doesn't it? Yet this sort of assertion is frequently made by human beings about other human beings of a different racial background. Is penguin-speak the solution to our problems?

Clearly it is not. Yet another language *is* the solution to our problems. It is the language of common humanity, the language of acceptance, of sharing, of equality and of reconciliation. This language doesn't use words. This language is heard in our smile, our choice of who we sit with to eat lunch and what jokes we laugh at and what jokes we don't.

Penelope Baker

1 Underline the topic sentence that is a **rhetorical question**.

2 In which sentence does the speaker first mention the topic? ______________________

3 Insert the missing letters. Paragraph 1 uses h _ _ _ _ _ to capture audience attention.

4 Paragraph 2 gains audience agreement with two words. What are they? ______________________ ______________________

5 Insert the missing letters. Sentence 5 of the last paragraph gives c _ _ _ _ _ _ _ examples of the i _ _ _ _ referred to in sentence 3.

Word usage

Be very careful of homonyms, words that sound the same but are spelt differently and have different meanings.

1 Underline the correct alternatives.

a Harry could here/hear the drone of a plane.

b Shelly Beach is pretty. Let's go there/their.

c Where/Wear are you travelling?

d Who's/Whose umbrella is that?

e There/They're/Their all stranded by floodwaters.

f They left their boots hear/here.

g Have you got your/you're books?

h They're/Their relatives live in Queensland.

i Whose/Who's lost this red pen?

2 Insert one of the following:

they're, their, there, whose, who's, hear, here, wear, where, you're

a Lifesavers risk ______________________ lives to save the careless and the weak.

b We store the basketballs in ______________________.

c Wobbegong sharks lurk down ______________________ at the bottom of the reef.

d High-rise window cleaners, ______________________ work is dangerous, ______________________ safety harnesses.

e Can you ______________________ the foghorns of the ships in the harbour?

f We saw yabbies down ______________________ in that rock pool.

g Do you have a zoom lens on ______________________ camera?

h The old blind dog did not know ______________________ he was going.

i Every girl ______________________ interested in playing tag should line up over ______________________.

Quick think

1 Using the Latin word *arbor* (tree) make words meaning:

a tree-dwelling arbor _ _ _

b botanical tree garden arbor _ _ _ _

c shady garden corner arb _ _ _

2 Underline the one that is not a tree.

a eucalypt **b** oak **c** larch **d** ash **e** sycamore **f** rattan **d** teak

3 Insert the missing letters. Teak logs are shifted by an elephant. The elephant is driven by its m _ _ _ _ t.

4 **a** Arrange these from smallest to largest in size: tree, plant, shrub.

____

b Arrange these in order of height: forest, grasslands, scrub.

____

c Plants are *native* to Australia or *exotic* (imported from other countries). Circle the exotic plant in this list.

wattle waratah eucalyptus scotch thistle boronia

d Circle the synonym (word with the same meaning) for *shrub*.

i plant **ii** flower **iii** cutting **iv** bush

Proofreading

Correct the spelling, usage and punctuation.

The elegy for fred bates was delivered by his son, Charlie who's succes in Sydney as a crimnal lawyer had always given him grate pride. Fred was never short of words himself and had always told charlie

'don't goble like a turkey. Speak clearly They have to here you rite down there at the back of the room.'

Charlie did his father preoud at the funeral. He spoke so well people wept wear they sat and did not hide there tiers.

Idiom

Explain:

1 Don't try to pull the wool over my eyes. ______________________________

2 The poor fellow was running on empty by the time he got here. ______________________________

Writing paragraphs and whole texts

'The Simpsons have a lot to answer for.'

1 Write a humorous introductory paragraph for the topic, using the framework below. Use your own paper.

a Rhetorical question

b Straight answer

c Statement covering concrete and absurd examples of Simpsons' influence

d Restatement of topic with emphasis

2 Draw up a plan for a speech which makes five points in favour of the argument: 'That drivers over 50 years of age should have to resit the driving test'. (Don't forget: humour and concrete examples.)

____

3 These sentences are all unsuitable for use in a speech. Why? Choose a reason for each being unsuitable from the adjectives below.

i too long **ii** wordy **iii** too casual **iv** ill-mannered **v** vague **vi** technical (boring)

— **a** Gee, it took a long time to prepare this. Well, here goes, anyway.

— **b** The giant panda, scientifically known as *Ailuropoda melanoleuca*, is the sole member of the genus and belongs to the family Ailuropodidae.

— **c** Ladies and Gents, I'm supposed to talk to you about crime statistics so let's get settled and get it over with.

— **d** From the time children bet an Icy Pole on the outcome of a game of marbles till the time, as retirees, they're betting on superannuation keeping them in the manner to which they have become accustomed, Australians are gambling—in the home, in clubs, on sporting fields.

— **e** Trust is one of those things like truth and justice—it just sort of is—you know when it's not there—it's what you could call an idea.

4 Write a humorous three-minute talk 'I wish I were a snake' to entertain a Year 7 class.

____

____

____

____

____

____

5 Write a list of reasons for the SRC to explain why Year 8 students should have lunchtime access to the computer room. Write an attention-getting introduction to the list and end it with a restatement of the need for that access.

____

____

____

____

____

____

Chapter test

1 Both the introduction and the conclusion of a speech should state the point of the speech.
Is this statement true or false? ____________

2 Which is the correct word to fill the gap in this sentence, *address* or *appeal*?
The Premier made an ____________ to everyone to contribute to a flood relief fund.

3 Mark ✗ wherever there should be a full stop in this sentence.
Capt James Cook mapped the east coast of Australia

4 Strike out the word with an incorrect capital letter.
The Victoria Cross is Australia's highest Award for military valour.

CHAPTER 2

Short story

STRUCTURE

in the beginning the caver is dominant; in the end the cave is dominant; the structure is planned around the stages of the changeover

introduction (brief) sets story in location and atmosphere

stage 1 of plot: reasoned response to being trapped

stage 2 of plot: macabre nature of cave—terror of cave—mind begins to go

stage 3 of plot: cave takes over—caver is simply still and traumatised—bones assume major role in story

conclusion (brief) closes action; raises the question only the reader can solve—what happened?

Bones

The tunnel stretched away into blackness. I tried turning my head to see the way I had come, but the cave walls were too constricting. I had to keep going. The tunnel felt as though it was getting narrower. I wriggled along, getting up momentum. Suddenly I ground to a halt. Too small, or too fat, depending on your perspective.

I twisted against the slimy walls; pushing forwards, backwards, any way that looked possible. I continued to struggle. I could feel a thousand little sand devils jabbing their tridents into my lungs. Then I burst through in a rush as the mud caked on the walls gave way. My lamp beam spun in crazy circles as I tumbled over an edge; falling with a thump into a soft sand base. I blinked. My light hit the opposite wall only fifteen feet from where I lay. Sitting up I rubbed the mud and grit out of my beard. The cave seemed to peter out, sloping into a hollow opposite me. I tried standing up but fell over immediately. My knee was twisted out of shape and refused to support me. I looked up. The ridge I had slid over was at least twelve feet above me. Careless potholer that I am, I knew that my rope would never be long enough to get me out.

I slumped back against the rock. Thoughts of all the cavers who had ever been trapped underground welled up in my mind. I tried to remember what had happened to them. I knew that some of the professionals had been rescued but the fate of the others eluded me. I switched my light off, remembering that Pete Johnson had done that and saved enough light to last several days. I ran my hand along the rock looking for a section more comfortable than the one I was sitting against. There wasn't any.

The cave smelt strange. Usually there's a musty, cold smell and the occasional reek of bat droppings. This chamber was almost odourless. The sand base was dry as well, not the muddy slime of the tunnel above. I couldn't fathom it. The cave was a freak of nature.

I dozed against the rock. I couldn't follow the passing of time underground, but I think it must have been several hours before I woke up. Turning on the lamp I cast its light idly around the chamber. Huddled into the hollow in the opposite wall there seemed to be a heap of white pebbles. I dragged myself over. Strange, long stones and others that were smaller, rounder. I started. Bones—leg bones, knuckles, ribs! I was back crushed into my rock in an instant.

Rivulets of terrified sweat poured from my face. Had someone else fallen into the cave languishing here forever in those bones; a stray animal; or something else that nobody knew about? I had no intention of waiting till they revealed themselves. Again I tried standing—agonising but not impossible. The rock face leading to the tunnel seemed higher and smoother than ever ... reaching for a tiny outcrop with my hand, I tried to scramble up before my knee had time to protest. I slid down. In feverish desperation I tried again and again. Behind me something giggled. The rock face disappeared and I fell against the floor.

When I woke it was to reassuring silence. My lamp had rolled across the floor when I fainted. Cautiously I reached across and snatched it back. The carbide was running out. Hardly daring to breathe I flashed the beam over the bones. A knuckle gleamed dully white. The light sputtered and died.

The darkness jostled me as I lay against the comforting solidity of my rock; pushing, shoving, teasing. I froze. Dead silence. Guffaws attacked me from all directions, outflanking my defences. Deep rumbling laughter assaulted me through the slab dark. In absolute terror I fumbled for the light, shaking and banging it, begging for a single spark ... nothing. I threw it against the wall. It blinked and I pounced on it, turning the winking light on the bones.

Silence. A tiny curl of dust twisted over the pile of bones.

I kept the light on them, my breathing fogging the air in front of me. Nothing happened; no sound, no movement, nothing ... the lamplight flashed and then disappeared. I shivered violently.

The cave was quiet for so long I began to calm down. I wondered how long it would take for them to find me ... I hadn't heard anyone calling or crashing about in the tunnel. There was no food and nothing to drink. I huddled against the rock now slippery with sweat.

The bones were whispering, confabulating about raspy secrets in their corner of the chamber. I stirred then slumped back against the rock. There was no light and nothing I could do ... I wondered again where they came from, these bones. The thought that they weren't really there even wormed its way into my mind. The gravelly whispering became fainter, almost expectant.

The cave sand seemed to have penetrated my brain, creating sandstorms that tore through destroying everything in their path. I closed my eyes. I felt drawn toward the bones—I knew them and they knew me. The sandstorms settled into soft dunes. My head fell forward and my hand slipped into the sand.

A sigh echoed around the cave. Was it me or was it the bones? Or was it both of us?

Angeline Baker

LANGUAGE FEATURES

topic sentences: short, varied, set subjects for their paragraphs

images based on sense response—smell of cave, sliminess of walls, dryness of sand—allow reader to share caver's experience

vivid and compact phrases

cause/response—two short balanced sentences underline horror of finding

rhetorical question *—puts us in caver's mind to share his thoughts*

verb 'giggled' conveys sense of unhealthy atmosphere, even of evil

battle metaphor emphasises power of cave over caver's mind

final sentence attention-getting contrast to previous pattern of nothing

neat connection with earlier smoothness—emphasises fear

's' sound underlines silence and 'power' of sand over his mind

questions turn horror into mystery

Comprehension

1 Underline the correct answer. The narrator was a victim of:

a a short rope **b** his own negligence **c** a caving accident

2 A *potholer* is one who:

a explores open caves **b** enters caves through potholes in a road

c enters caves through a sinkhole in the ground.

3 Underline the incorrect answer.

a The actual tunnel was narrow. **b** The caver was too fat.

c The tunnel was narrowed by caked mud.

4 Find one piece of evidence that the story is set in the first part of the twentieth century.

____

5 Underline what distinguished this cave from all other caves.

a its sandy base **b** the bones **c** its lack of odour

6 The guffaws this potholer heard were:

a quiet giggles **b** raucous laughter **c** happy chuckles

7 Why do you think the potholer found silence 'reassuring'?

____

8 Underline the most satisfactory explanation of what happened to this caver.

a The darkness attacked and killed him. **b** The bones attacked and killed him.

c His mind gave way under the strain of terror. **d** The sand smothered him.

Writing skills

1 Insert the following in the blanks: identification, first, subject.

This story is written in the ______________ person to increase the reader's ______________ with the ______________ of the story.

2 This story deals with the unnatural. What part of this story first suggests the unusual? ______________

____

3 Which word in the first topic sentence suggests the unknown? ______________

4 The writer uses a simile/metaphor to convey the caver's inability to get enough air in paragraph 2. Underline it in the story. Is it a simile or a metaphor? ______________

5 What verb conveys the first proof that something is seriously and abnormally wrong with this cave?

____

6 Underline the reason that *giggled* is more effective than *laughed* or *screamed*?

a It is a good word. **b** The other two words are too noisy. **c** It suggests something unhealthy.

7 Which sentence first indicates that the caver is now resigned to his fate?

____

8 Underline the correct answer. The atmosphere of this story could best be described as:

a dramatic **b** tense **c** chilling **d** spooky

9 The image the writer uses to describe what is going on in the potholer's mind is an image of:

a a desert **b** a sandstorm **c** a sandstorm in a desert

10 What part of the image shows that the potholer's mind is no longer functioning?

a the sand entering his brain **b** the sand destroying his brain function

c his mind settling into 'soft dunes'

11 Underline the correct answer. The story's ending is effective because it is the logical end for:

a a madman's story

b a story with the theme of the unknown

c a story going nowhere

Vocabulary

discrete	**canvass**	**compliment**	**affect**	**supersonic**
discreet	**canvas**	**complement**	**effect**	**supernatural**

All these words are very commonly confused. Take care to learn to use them correctly and to spell them. A good way to remember the first two is to imagine the letter 'e' is a secret—the *discreet* person keeps his secrets locked up inside, but a chatterbox scatters them around so they are *discrete*—all over the place and separated.

Focus on punctuation

Paragraphs

Mark new paragraphs ([ ) in the following. (Remember: ideas, action and speech paragraphs.)

My mind went off at a tangent. I opened the drawer of my desk where I'd left Gustav's charm. I pulled it out, and tossed the bullet and its broken silver chain in front of Mr Dickson. 'Have you seen this, Mr ah-hmm Dickson?' He slowly reached out to pick up the object. He held it close to his eyes then gave a smile. I said, to prompt him, 'Russell told me this was Gustav's lucky charm. It's a parabellum bullet—out of a German machine gun.' That extra information was superfluous. Mr Dickson smiled again. 'It may be Gustav's charm, but it's not a parabellum bullet.'

(Extract from *Too Old for Murder* by Kevin Baker, Reid Books, Wyong, NSW, 1996)

Select a word

Find adjectives to mean:

1 easily broken (glass/china) f _ _ _ _ _ e

2 easily broken (bone/twigs) b _ _ _ _ _ e

3 weak, slow-moving f _ _ _ _ e

4 weak, lightweight f _ _ _ l

5 moving m _ b _ _ e

6 not moving i _ _ _ b _ _ e

7 wise, careful p _ _ d _ _ t

8 unwise or rash i _ _ _ _ d _ _ t

Grammar

Compound sentences and relative clauses

- **Compound sentences** contain two or more **simple sentences** of equal importance. Simple sentences can be joined to make a compound sentence by words like *and, but, so, then, or*. These are called **coordinate conjunctions**, e.g.
  James is Jack's elder brother and Peter is his younger brother.
- **Complex sentences** contain one important sentence (called a **main clause**) and one or more less important sentences (called **dependent clauses**). Main clauses and dependent clauses are joined to make a complex sentence using words like *because, when, after, unless, until, although, as, while, before, whenever, wherever*. These are called **subordinate conjunctions**, e.g.
  I am very tired because I ran four laps around the oval.
- Simple sentences or main clauses make sense by themselves, e.g. *I am very tired.* Dependent clauses do not, e.g. *because I ran four laps around the oval.*

1 Write 'compound' or 'complex' beside each sentence.

a Hamid wanted to go roller-blading but Eddie wanted to go swimming. __________

b Rachel plays the violin and her sister plays the oboe. __________

c Harry is a good footballer because he is very fast on his feet. __________

d The fish were biting until the sky became overcast. __________

2 Underline the main clause in each sentence.

a Charlie will not bat until the bowler changes.

b The vet stroked the cat so it settled down quickly.

c Although lightning flashed angrily they were safe in the deep cave.

d Unless you hold the ladder for me I will not climb onto the roof.

3 Underline the dependent clauses in each sentence.

a When the sand bar collapsed all the swimmers had to swim for their lives.

b Do not swim outside the flags because those areas are not patrolled by lifesavers.

c If you cannot see the bottom, never dive into a river.

d Everyone rushed out of the water when the shark alarm sounded.

4 Write 'main' (clause) or 'dependent' (clause) to name the underlined clauses.

a I want to go to Sea World but my sister wants to go to Movie World. ______________

b Until you return my ball I will keep the racquet. ______________

c Wherever Leila walked her cat followed her. ______________

d You have to shut the gate or the sheep will escape. ______________

Word study

1 Underline the correct alternative.

a Members of parliament should canvas/canvass the ideas of their constituents.

b Telling me I sing like a kookaburra is no compliment/complement.

c Sunburn can have a serious effect/affect on your health in later life.

d Jane can always keep a confidence. She is very discrete/discreet.

e We will have to waterproof our tent canvas/canvass again.

2 Match column A with column B.

A		**B**	
a	tactful	**i**	complement
b	completing part	**ii**	canvas
c	tarpaulin	**iii**	discreet
d	result	**iv**	discrete
e	change	**v**	effect
f	separate	**vi**	affect

3 The Latin word *super* means above or over. It is often used as a prefix, e.g. *supernatural* (not of the natural world). Using the prefix *super~*, make words meaning:

a	extremely critical	superc _ _ _ _ _ _ l
b	not needed	superf _ _ _ _ s
c	beyond human capacity	superh _ _ _ n
d	large self-service shop	superm _ _ _ _ t
e	greater than the speed of sound	supers _ _ _ c

Word usage

1 Insert the following words in the blanks:

shot, add, inquired, condition, legendary, approached, birth, urgency

THE GHAN

In the old days, the Ghan was **a**____________________ for its delays. Floods could **b**____________________ days to the journey. On one occasion, John said, the train had been stuck in one place for several days and one of the women on board **c**____________________ the conductor.
'When are we getting to Alice Springs?' she **d**____________________.
'Madam how should I know?' he replied.
'But you can see this is a matter of **e**____________________. I am to give **f**____________________ any day now,' said the woman.
'Well, Madam, a woman in your **g**____________________ has no business travelling on the Ghan,' said the conductor.
'Well, I wasn't in this condition when I left Adelaide,' **h**____________________ back the woman.

2 Insert the missing letters. A very short story such as 'The Ghan' is called an an _ _ d _ t e. It is usually entertaining, interesting and spoken rather than written.

3 Some words are used so often they become worn out from overuse and lose their effect. The use of such overworked words spoils otherwise good writing. Overworked words include *nice*, *ultimate*, *legendary* and *fantastic*. Replace the word *nice* with appropriate words from below. Do not use any word twice.

sky, rotund, pretty, generous, unique, accurate, enamelled, impolite

a Paolo is a nice fellow. He'd give anyone a hand. ____________________

b My parents gave me a nice birthday present. I love it. ____________________

c Cassandra wore a nice blue shirt on the picnic. ____________________

d Anthea's nice earrings were lost in the beach sand. ____________________

4 Replace the <u>overworked</u> words with more appropriate words.

a I've scratched my favourite CD. What a <u>disaster!</u> ______________________

b That was a <u>legendary</u> party. ______________________

c This is the <u>ultimate</u> in new car design. ______________________

5 In formal writing it is best to avoid **colloquialisms**, e.g. *Joe was <u>a bit of a dag</u>*. Replace the underlined colloquialisms with formal expressions.

a He wears <u>cool gear</u>. ______________________

b She looks <u>dorky</u> in that clown suit. ______________________

c They <u>nicked me runners</u> so I <u>dobbed them in</u>. ______________________

____

Quick think

1 Complete the following words on caves and cave life.

a the study of caves	sp _ _ _ _ _ ogy
b one who studies caves	sp _ _ _ _ _ _ _ ist
c a vertical tunnel in a cave system	sh _ _ t
d the bottom of a cave	f _ _ _ r
e totally cave-dwelling	subt _ _ _ _ _ _ an

2 Write adjectives to describe the following:

a damp stale air	d _ _ k
b a poorly lit unpleasant atmosphere	g _ _ _ _ y
c a confined atmosphere that feels suffocating	cl _ _ s t _ _ p h _ b _ _
d unable to solve a mystery	m _ _ _ _ f _ _ d
e so frightened you can't move	p _ t _ _ f _ _ d

Proofreading

Correct the spelling.

Loud noise over extended periods can effect yor hearing. Music chanelled directly into the ear via earphones damiges oral sensitivity. When naturally loud music is complimented by volume controles set on maximum, damage is certin and permanint. Too many poeple do not relize that there hereing is a very delicate mechanism until it's two late. Most poeple do not know their deaf until sumone says 'Turn that radio down. I can't hear myself think.'

Idiom

Explain:

1 Let's run it up the flagpole and see what people think. ______________________

____

2 Mike's only a fair-weather friend. ______________________

____

Writing paragraphs and whole texts

1 Arrange the following paragraph ideas into a logical order for a short story entitled 'Ambushed'.

______ **a** Ultimatum: Bin cigarettes or be dobbed in.

______ **b** Senior student alerts SRC representative for Year 8.

______ **c** Representative confronts wagging smokers.

______ **d** Two Year 8 students plan to wag period 6 to smoke.

______ **e** Representative waits by hole in fence.

______ **f** Senior student overhears plan while practising HSC music assessment piece.

______ **g** Two waggers meet at bottom of stairwell and set off for fence.

2 Write a short topic sentence for each of the above paragraphs. Vary the sentence structure and start with a different word each time.

a ______________________

b ______________________

c ______________________

d ______________________

e ______________________

f ______________________

g ______________________

3 Write a joke you have heard as a humorous anecdote. Keep it brief (one paragraph) and make the punchline your final sentence. Make sure you have a simple, direct topic sentence.

____

____

____

____

____

____

____

4 Write an introductory paragraph to a short story about a midnight prowler. Make sure you create a midnight atmosphere. (Consider what your senses tell you about midnight.) Make your topic sentence set the atmosphere.

____
____
____
____
____
____
____
____

5 Write a concluding paragraph to a story about a lost child. Make sure you let the reader know what has happened and the reactions of those concerned.

____
____
____
____
____
____
____
____
____
____

Chapter test

1 The topic or first sentence in each paragraph of a story should vary in length and structure.

True/false? ____________

2 Which is the correct word to fill the space? discrete/discreet?

He carefully placed the __________ shapes into one complete jigsaw puzzle.

3 What joining word would you use to link these two sentences in one compound sentence?

Myfi went skating this afternoon. Her friend Amy accompanied her. ________

4 Circle any words in the list that could replace the word *nice* in this sentence.

Wally wore his favourite nice shirt.

torn, colourful, striped, tattered, canvas, smelly, smart

CHAPTER 3

Newspaper report

STRUCTURE

headline

introduction—
- *main fact of report*
- *origin of story*

body of story—
2 parts:
- *the problem*
- *the solution*

conclusion

Crossword puzzle solves puzzle of old lady's will

LONDON: The crossword editor of the *Daily Telegraph* (English) has helped solve the puzzle over an elderly woman's will.

When Annetta Duel died in May at the age of 99, her family could find no will. But then her nephew, Leonard Andren, came across an envelope in which she left all her worldly belongings to him—in a scrawled message on the side of a *Daily Telegraph* crossword.

Above her signature Mrs Duel had written: 'I leave all my possessions to Len and I hope he will be happy as long as he lives. God bless you. Aunty Nettie, goodbye.'

The space above the adjacent clues carried the words 'Don't throw this away please.'

The problem: The will was not dated, and Mr Andren's lawyer said it was not valid if it could not be determined when it was written.

Enter the *Daily Telegraph*'s Val Gilbert.

'The will was written beside the crossword, but that was literally all there was to it,' Ms Gilbert said. 'Luckily, I have quite a good filing system here, so I was able to look up the number of that crossword 22 515, and show that it appeared on June 8 last year.'

'I quite like the idea that this old lady was doing the crossword right up until the end. Good on her!' Gilbert said.

The crossword editor said that Mr Andren's lawyer advised that, since it was properly signed, Mrs Duel's will did not have to be witnessed by a third party.

It will be considered valid if no later document is found.

The size of the estate was not disclosed.

The *Daily Telegraph* (Australia)

LANGUAGE FEATURES

play with word 'puzzle'

- *very short paragraphs—1 or 2 sentences only*
- *simple vocabulary so all can read it*
- *factual writing—what happened, nothing else*

very simple statement of problem with use of colon

direct speech (quotations) lends note of authenticity and adds a human dimension to a legal problem

indirect speech

formal legal phrasing gives note of seriousness to a simple human interest story

Comprehension

1 When did Mrs Duel die? ____________________

2 Where did Mrs Duel write her will? ____________________

3 Underline the correct answer. Her will was validated by:

a her own signature **b** the date of the crossword **c** both of these

4 How do we know that Mrs Duel was of sound mind when she wrote her will?

____

5 Underline the correct answer. Val Gilbert is:

a nephew to Mrs Duel **b** Andren's lawyer **c** a crossword editor

6 Explain how Val Gilbert validated Mrs Duel's will. ______________________________

____

7 Mrs Duel wrote her will when she was dying. Is this true or false? __________________

8 What is the value of Andren's inheritance? __________________

9 What do you think would happen if another, later will was found? __________________

____

Writing skills

1 The headline plays on two meanings of the word *puzzle*. What are they?

a ______________________________ **b** ______________________________

2 Insert the missing word. Such word play is called a p___n.

3 Underline the correct answer. The word *LONDON* at the beginning of the text establishes:

a the headquarters of the *Daily Telegraph*

b the origin of the story

c the location of the editor's office

4 The main point of the story is first revealed in paragraph 7. Is this true or false? __________________

5 Underline the correct answer. Val Gilbert's words convey:

a fact **b** fact and opinion **c** opinion

6 Underline the correct answer. Gilbert's comment 'Good on her!' suggests:

a She admires Mrs Duel.

b She approves of keeping the mind occupied always.

c She is surprised by Mrs Duel's mental capacity at 99.

7 This story has two parts separated by paragraph 5. What does each part deal with?

______________________________ ______________________________

8 What verb tells us that Mrs Duel did not carefully compose the wording of her will? __________________

9 Why is *Daily Telegraph* written in italics? ______________________________

Vocabulary

adherence	**adapt**	**adverse**	**already**	**access**
adhesion	**adopt**	**averse**	**all ready**	**excess**

These pairs of words are all commonly confused, usually because people are unsure of their spelling. After you have established their different meanings in the following activities, learn to spell them using the Look, Cover, Write, Check method.

Focus on punctuation

Apostrophe of possession

- An **apostrophe** indicates ownership. It immediately follows the owner's name and is itself followed by 's', e.g.
  John's book is lost.
- If the singular owning noun ends in 's' then you can do one of two things: add *'s* as usual or just place an apostrophe after the last 's' of the word, e.g.
  Chris's or *Chris'*
- If the owner is a plural and already ends in 's', the apostrophe simply follows the owner alone, e.g.
  The footballers' jerseys were dirty.
- Sometimes only the owner's name is included, not what is owned. The apostrophe is still placed immediately after the owner and an 's' is added, e.g.
  She left her shoes at the bootmaker's.

1 Insert the apostrophe in these singular word groups.
- **a** Henrys horse, the mechanics spanner, a praying mantiss wings
- **b** the teams loss, a lonely birds cry, an audiences enthusiasm

2 Insert the apostrophe in these plural word groups.
- **a** ships cats, guitars strings, girls jeans
- **b** mens hats, geeses yard, sheeps trough

3 Insert the missing apostrophes.
- **a** Ethiopian Abebe Bikilas consecutive marathon wins made Olympic history.
- **b** Mr Williams firm deals in American skateboards.
- **c** A gooses loud honk is an excellent deterrent to trespassers.
- **d** Ben Lomas peak was shrouded in mist.

Select a word

Choose synonyms from the vocabulary list for:

1 hostile ____________________ **2** unwilling ____________________

3 improvise ____________________ **4** grip ____________________

5 surplus ____________________ **6** prepared ____________________

Grammar

Subject–verb agreement

- If a subject is singular (only one), the verb form must be singular too.

  If the subject is plural (more than one), the verb form must be plural too, e.g.
  Irena and her friends are going shopping.
  Plural subject Plural verb form

  Peter is inside the boatshed.
  Singular subject Singular verb form
- If a subject is a collective noun the verb is generally singular, e.g.
  The herd stampeded because lightning struck in its paddock.
  Collective noun Singular verb

1 Underline the subject of the verb in each sentence. Write S (singular) or P (plural) to describe its number.

a The flag flapped wildly in the wind. __

b Sailors are lining the decks in ranked order __

c The orchestra tuned its instruments at the start of the concert. __

d Farmers and their dogs all enjoy sheep dog trials. __

2 Underline the correct verb.

a Eleven cricketers and their reserve has/have fallen ill.

b The League team is/are drawn to play Siding Springs tomorrow.

c The Hockeyroos is/are our most successful international sports players.

d Candidates for election as school captain is/are required to nominate by 3 pm on Friday.

3 Read these sentences carefully. Underline any incorrect verbs.

a The two boys have done their homework and is now listening to CDs.

b The team's manager plans nightly training but the team disagree.

c Damage to marine life and our foreshores from an oil spill at sea are almost immeasurable.

Word study

1 Find words from the vocabulary list to fill the blanks.

a The ______________________ effects of smoking are well-known.

b The motocross heats had ______________________ ended when the supercross bikes were still being registered.

c ______________________ food from the sausage sizzle will go to the school chooks.

d Some craft glues lack ______________________ for plastics work.

2 Underline the correct alternative.

a Wheelchair access/excess is rare at pop concerts.

b Most school SRCs adapt/adopt a code of rules for council meetings.

c The ingredients were already/all ready for use when the cooking class arrived.

d Historically people have died rather than give up adherence/adhesion to their religious beliefs.

3 Tick the sentences where the underlined word is correct. Cross (✗) the sentences where the underlined word is wrong and write the correct word in the space.

a Animals without young will sometimes adapt an orphaned baby. __ __________

b He was adverse to running in any conditions at all. __ __________

c I had all ready eaten because I was so hungry. __ __________

d There is no free excess to that swimming pool. __ __________

e You need a dry surface for paint to have good adhesion. __ __________

Evaluating other people's writing

Floods havoc

Residents of two north coast towns remain isolated by floods after three days of heavy rain.

Families in Birdwood, near Taree, have been left stranded after the bridge across the Hastings River was washed away yesterday morning.

State emergency service volunteers are attempting to reach the families.
about 100 mid-north coast residents were evacuated last week after eight rivers burst their banks.

SES volunteers have also made food drops by boat to the town of Bobin on the Manning River after the river burst its banks.

Sydney residents devastated by April's hailstorm were also affected during the week. The SES received more than 1300 calls for help, mostly to secure tarpaulins.

The *Daily Telegraph* [Australia]

Read the report above carefully and answer the following.

1 Underline the correct answer. *Havoc* in this headline means:

a chaos **b** destruction **c** damage **d** disorder **e** confusion

2 *Isolated* has a synonym in paragraph 2. What is it? ______________________________

3 What word means *unpaid workers*? ____________________

4 Underline the correct answer. The expression *burst their banks* means:

a eroded their banks **b** overflowed their banks

5 Insert the missing word. The expression *burst their banks* is used twice. Such ____________________ is an instance of poor writing.

6 Underline the correct answer. *Secure tarpaulins* here means:

a find tarpaulins **b** tie down tarpaulins **c** store tarpaulins safely

Word usage

- Neither/nor and either/or are singular patterns, so they are always followed by a singular verb form, e.g.
  Neither your father nor I approves of your staying out late.
- Phrases containing a singular class/group word (*style, sort, kind, manner, box* etc.) also take a singular verb form. If they are plural they take a plural form. This can be tricky. Be careful, e.g.
  This kind of hat does not suit me. These kinds of hats are old-fashioned. This box of nails and screws is heavy.

1 Underline the correct alternatives.

a Neither his brother or/nor he could attend.

b This sort of accident is/are too frequent on our beaches.

c That style of swimmers is/are very fashionable this summer.

d Either Gillian or/nor her sister was/were present.

2 Insert the correct verb form.

a Either your brother or I ________________ ('to be') certain to be here.

b That parcel of books and papers ________________ (past of 'to be') going to be burned.

c That manner of fooling around and joking ________________ ('to be') likely to get him into trouble.

d Neither the red book nor the green one ________________ (past of 'to be') to be found.

3 Circle the correct verb in each sentence.

a These kinds of games is/are too drawn out for me.

b That sort of pig is/are called a Berkshire pig.

c The Captain's sea chest full of ocean charts were/was lost when his ship sank.

d A pair of scissors are/is not what I asked you to buy; I wanted a pair of secateurs.

Quick think

Do you know newspaper terminology? Match the term to its meaning.

1 headline _____	**a** a completed batch of printing
2 by-line _____	**b** self-employed journalist
3 editorial _____	**c** bold title summing up contents
4 commentary _____	**d** news report in photographs only
5 investigative journalism _____	**e** column by editor on topical issue
6 editor _____	**f** correct text and layout supervisor
7 subeditor _____	**g** signature of reporter on item
8 print run _____	**h** researched story reporting
9 in-house journalist _____	**i** regular discussion feature
10 freelance journalist _____	**j** journalist employed by publishing company
11 photo-journalism _____	**k** responsible for overall contents and production of newspaper

Proofreading

Correct apostrophes, agreements and vocabulary choice.

Paulines' friend was adverse to visiting the zoo on an excursion. 'All those sort of animals are on science videos all ready,' she complained.

After a coffee at Antonias she admitted she actually liked going to see the zoos' creatures but she hated the access of walking you had to do there.

Idiom

Explain:

1 I always keep ten dollars for a rainy day. ________________________________

____

2 She walks around with her nose in the air. ________________________________

____

Writing paragraphs and whole texts

1 The headline is composed by the subeditor. Compose headlines for these stories. Remember:

- Be precise
- Omit unnecessary words.
- Play on word meanings if you can.

a A sparrow has hatched two chicks in the ice-cream tub where old John Harvey kept his savings. The tub was on a back-verandah shelf.

____

b Workers at a chicken-processing plant went on strike because it was too hot in the plant. They want cooling and extractor fans installed before they go back to work.

____

c Popular local recording artist, Andy Murray, whose latest song is 'Iced Blue', was slightly injured while on a skiing holiday in Switzerland. A heavy piece of ice sliding from a chalet roof struck his shoulder as he walked towards the chairlift.

____

2 The first paragraph contains the main point of the news story. It must be direct, factual and dramatic. Choose one of the stories above and write the first paragraph of a news report.

____

____

____

____

____

3 Using the details in the box below and your own paper, write a newspaper report about the incident. Remember, news reports have a special layout and style of writing. Make sure you include in your report: headline, column layout (if more than 100 words), story's origin, short factual paragraphs, and quotations from witnesses/authority figures.

a	Jetski flipped by wave at Tamarama	**b**	Male jetski driver, 19, injured
c	Swimmers in area	**d**	Driver + one swimmer rescued by lifesavers
e	Driver, ambulance to hospital	**f**	Swimmer, helicopter to hospital Spinal Unit
g	Jetski retrieved by swimmers		

Chapter test

1 Newspaper stories are written in large paragraphs of several sentences. True or false? ____________

2 Tick the words with apostrophes correctly placed. Cross (✗) those that are not.

a the tiger's four paws _____
b the three black hens' eggs _____
c the yellow teams' goals _____
d Mr Harris' hat _____
e Elsies' ballet shoes _____

3 The following sentence is grammatically correct. True or false? ____________

Ben, Fuad, Mike and Gino plus Mike's dog is down by the creek.

4 Circle the correct verb.

Neither Caitlin nor Serena are/is in the classroom yet.

CHAPTER 4

Advertisement

STRUCTURE

A*—designed to* <u>*sell*</u> *a product:*
- *design reflects product*
- *design includes* <u>*fact*</u> *and* <u>*inducement*</u>

heading (product)

subheading (explanation of product)

major selling point

layout: separator line (incorporated cleverly into advertisement here)

persuasion and inducement

small print facts and conditions

LANGUAGE FEATURES

A*—minimal text and large white space suggest carefree holidays*

word choice of a superlative emphasises extreme happiness

question—to make the idle reader take notice

statement of fact

instruction designed to evoke response: stop, listen, act

details in note form

B*—selling point is product attraction*

- *product + basic facts*

persuasion and inducements

small print facts and conditions

border drawn as mapped trek starting and ending with product vendor, Peregrine Travel

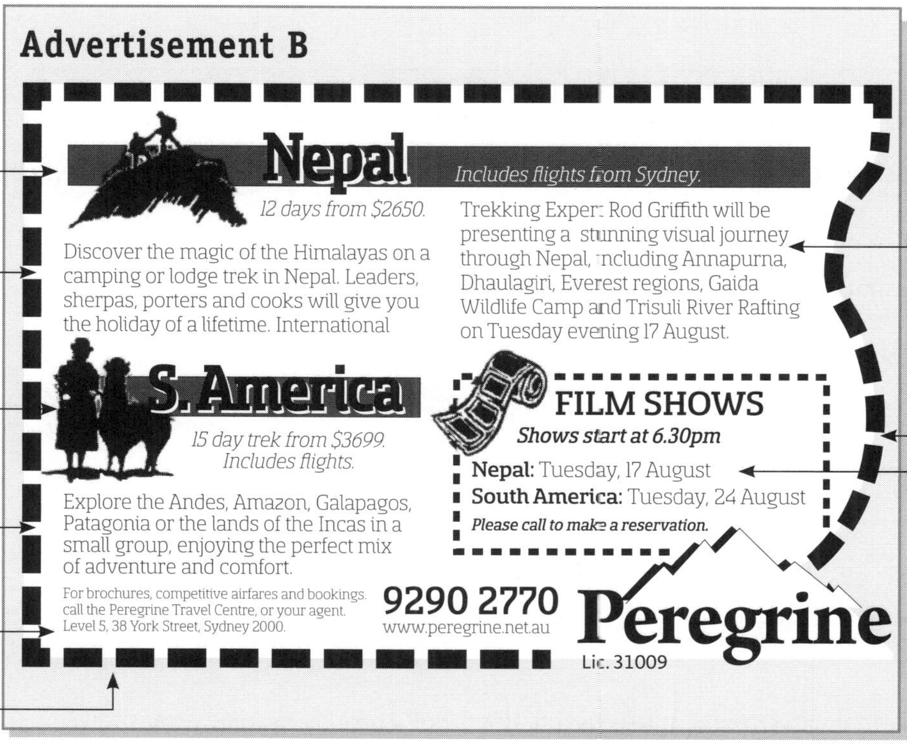

B*—formal sentences using:*
- *evocative words (names, places)*
- *imperative mood; e.g. 'discover, explore'*
- *historical allusion*

details—brief, condensed

Comprehension

Advertisement A

1 Where will you holiday in Thailand with this package deal? ______________________

2 Evening meals are included in the deal. Is this true or false? ______________________

3 $999 is the fixed price of this holiday package. Is this true or false? ______________________

4 Do these prices apply to holiday-makers from Adelaide? ______________________

Advertisement B

5 Peregrine Travel offers three modes of contact with its staff. These are:

______________________ ______________________ ______________________

6 One could expect 5-star hotel accommodation on Peregrine Tours. Is this true or false? ______________

7 The Nepal Tour leaves on 17 August. Is this true or false? ______________________

8 Underline the correct answer. Peregrine tours are:

a coach tours **b** adventure tours **c** cultural tours

Writing skills

Advertisement A

1 Underline the correct answer. The words *Thailand Tropical Treats* are an example of:

a simile **b** alliteration **c** metaphor **d** comparison

2 The circle and rays around the price suggest two ideas, only one of which is related to the price.

What are they? ____

____

3 Insert the missing words. The palm tree line across the advertisement has a visual function, to encourage would-be customers to imagine **a** ________________________________, and a textual function, to separate **b** ________________________________.

4 The first question of the medium print is addressed to ______________________.

5 Insert missing letters. The advertiser here c _ _ t _ _ sts two situations.

6 Insert missing letters. The purpose here is to p _ _ _ _ _ de the reader to choose a warmer situation.

7 Which sentence of the small print is intended to <u>inform</u> the reader?

____

8 Underline one answer only. The sales pitch (advertising angle) of the advertisement is:

a cheap travel package **b** affordable escape **c** Pattaya Beach pleasures

Advertisement B

9 Which word in this advertisement tells us that this is not a holiday by luxury transport? ______________

10 Underline all correct answers. Words such as *Andes, Galapagos, Annapurna* and *Trisuli River* are intended to suggest which of the following ideas?

a remoteness **b** adventure **c** exotic scenery **d** conventional travel

e professionalism **f** challenge **g** superior travel arrangements

11 Underline the correct answer. Little emphasis is placed on price in this advertisement because:

a it is not the most important consideration for the target market

b financial details are not available

c the price would scare off potential customers

12 Underline the correct answer. The broken line outline of this advertisement represents:

a simply an advertisement frame **b** a trek's progress in South America

c a visual reinforcement of what the advertisement offers: trekking

13 Insert the missing letters. This advertisement and advertisement A are written and presented differently but their purpose is the same: to s _ _ _ a product.

Vocabulary

trek	**shuffle**	**trudge**	**stroll**	**amble**
politician	**diplomat**	**feasible**	**possible**	**necessary**

It is a good idea in Year 8 to begin keeping a notebook of useful vocabulary. This will help you write in a more interesting way because you will have a variety of words to say the same thing and to say precisely what you mean. (Look at all the different 'walk' words, in the top row above.) Don't forget to break words into syllables and use the Look, Cover, Write, Check method to learn the more difficult words.

Focus on punctuation

Full stops; question & exclamation marks

- A **full stop** ends a sentence and marks an abbreviation, e.g. *Mr Snow is absent.*
- A **question mark** ends a sentence that demands an answer, e.g. *Where is Mr Snow?*
- An **exclamation mark** ends a dramatic sentence, e.g. *Mr Snow is always absent!*
- A full stop ends a reported or indirect question, one that does not require an answer, e.g. *Shelley asked where Mr Snow was.*

1 Insert all missing full stops.

a Lt Col Christopher Sparks has been appointed to Holsworthy base

b Dr and Mrs Abramovitz will be attending the dinner hosted by Charles Coe, MLA

2 Add the missing end punctuation to these sentences.

a Are you going to the disco tonight

b The crowd roared its approval, 'Go, the Saints'

c Morrie asked whether the match had been cancelled

d Nina plays the violin as well as the piano

e Have you done your warm up exercises

3 Tick the correctly punctuated sentences and cross (✗) the incorrect ones.

a Where has he gone! __

b Unless she arrives soon we will go without her. __

c Why do some birds only eat on the wing? __

d The question was about whether eagles mate for life? __

4 Add question and exclamation marks where necessary.

a Why is this work incomplete Why, it's not even half-finished Finish it immediately

b To whom should I address this letter Bob His father His mother All of them together

5 Insert all missing punctuation.

How will we know if it's Rev Bill Smith, Dr Barry Howson or Corp Charlie Groves if they're all out of uniform Dashed if I know how we're supposed to know

Select a word

1 Choose a word to rhyme with the given verb from the vocabulary list. The word must match the meaning in brackets, e.g.

	trudge	(confuse, trick)	fudge
a	amble	(bet, wager)	______________
b	stroll	(cricket throw)	______________
c	shuffle	(breathe noisily)	______________
d	trek	(small spot or mark)	______________

2 Arrange these verbs according to the degree of effort expended, starting with the least effort.

heave, raise, lever, flip

least effort ______________________________ most effort

3 Make nouns out of these adjectives.

possible ______________ feasible ______________ necessary ______________

Grammar

Relative pronouns

Relative pronouns begin dependent clauses. They describe a noun in the main clause.

Relative pronouns are: *who, whom, whose, which, that*, e.g.

The black dog that saved Peter from drowning has been adopted by Peter's family.

Noun Relative pronoun Dependent clause

Relative pronouns in the wrong place confuse meaning, e.g.

Sam borrowed cricket gear from his mate who was sleeping. CORRECT

Noun Relative pronoun

Sam borrowed his mate's cricket gear who was sleeping. INCORRECT

Noun Relative pronoun

The second sentence is incorrect because the placing of the relative pronoun tells us that the gear was asleep.

1 Insert the appropriate relative pronoun.

a David enjoyed the fiery curry ______________________ the Shah family had prepared.

b Lucy, ______________________ ambition was to be a politician, spent a lot of time reading history.

c For Mrs Roberts, ______________________ is deaf and blind, the assistance of her guide dog makes shopping not only feasible but possible.

2 Join these sentences using a correctly positioned relative pronoun.

a Jim Kalamiotis is just one of the third generation of his family to go trawling. Jim's grandfather had been a prawn fisher back in the Greek Islands.

____

b Gareth Evans was a politician. He also became known as a statesman in world affairs.

____

3 Rewrite the following so that the relative pronouns are correctly placed.

a A yellow moon rose over the end of the street which smiled benignly as Nick practised his trumpet in the backyard.

____

b Under the bridge choked with traffic that arched over the harbour a slow tugboat chugged.

____

Word study

1 These list words have been scrambled. Can you work out what they are?

a IANLPOCITI ____________ **b** SBLEFIAE ____________

c RAYSESECN ____________ **d** SPBSIEOL ____________

2 Circle any of the following that could be described as *necessary* for human life.

shirts	air	meat	water
milk	jeans	houses	shelter
fish	grass	boats	food

3 Match an appropriate list 'walk' word from the vocabulary list to each of these walkers.

a an explorer crossing difficult terrain ____________

b a reluctant student going to school ____________

c an arthritic old person wearing slippers ____________

d someone walking on the beach at sunrise ____________

e someone window shopping to fill in time ____________

4 Underline the most appropriate word.

a International diplomacy requires the participation of a diplomat/politician.

b A site inspection report that construction of a skateboard ramp was possible/feasible on that piece of waste land, together with the sudden availability of funds, meant that it was now possible/feasible for council to proceed with construction plans.

5 Arrange the following in ascending order of necessity (smallest to greatest).

a necessary **b** wanted **c** needed **d** essential ______________________

____

Word usage

Armstrong, Hillary and Earhart all set off from the same spot

The next famous explorer may be sliding down the slippery dip. You just have to get your kid on the right track. Kidz.net is the first 'net' just for kids, with thousands of the world's best sites for curious minds. Click onto Education for subjects from kindy to Year 12. Click onto Metro and they can browse through aviator museums or find inspiration in an art gallery. Click onto sport and they'll find all their sporting heroes and winning techniques. Or, just for fun, they can download all their favourite action and strategy games. And, of course, there's a site for budding astronauts. It's so easy kids will actually want to learn. And that's a feat in itself. Kidz.net is also a safe place for kids. No violence, no porn. So there's no looking over their shoulders. To find Kidz.net around Australia get on the net with Telstra Big Pond Home. Then subscribe to Kidz.net for only $9.95 a month! You can even try Kidz.net for one month free. Just pick up your free CD Starter Pack at participating Telstra shops, Caltex or Ampol stores. And who knows, your little one may soon be climbing Everest. For more information on Kidz.net, call 1300 655 439.

(Advertisement from 1998, now outdated.)

Jargon is the vocabulary that is specific to a particular activity or area of knowledge and not commonly used in other circumstances; for example scientific jargon includes such words as *molecule* and *subatomic particle*, which are not used in everyday language.

1 **a** Underline three examples of computer jargon in this advertising text.

b Underline three examples of advertising jargon (words or phrases) in this text.

2 Underline the meaning which would best match the way the word is used in the advertising text.

a inspiration	**b** techniques	**c** action	**d** subscribe
i an idea	**i** ways	**i** sports	**i** belong
ii an impetus to artistic creativity	**ii** methods	**ii** player involvement	**ii** contribute
iii encouragement	**iii** means	**iii** deed	**iii** pay

3 Find words in the text that mean the following.

a inquisitive ______________________ **b** planning ______________________

c developing ______________________

Quick think

One of advertising's favourite words is *astronomical*, e.g. *astronomical savings* and *astronomical* bargains (meaning huge savings or bargains can be expected). The Greek word *astron* (star) is the base of many words such as *astronomical*.

1 Can you complete the following words based on *astron*?

a the study of stars a _ _ _ _ _ _ _ y **b** one who travels in space a _ _ _ _ _ _ _ t

c study of the physics of the universe a _ _ _ _ p _ _ _ _ _ s

d one who casts horoscopes a _ _ _ _ _ _ _ _ r

2 Match these people and their fields of study.

a astronomer _____ **i** roles of Cancer and Leo etc. in the universe

b astrologer _____ **ii** roles of white dwarves and black holes etc. in the universe

3 Match each example of jargon to its meaning, then write where it is used on the line. Don't forget to use your dictionary.

Jargon	Meaning	Where used
remote (noun)	**i** a place on a field	______________
ride-on (noun)	**ii** an operating control	______________
silly-mid-on (adverb)	**iii** to make a loop	______________
knot (noun)	**iv** a lawnmower	______________
tat (verb)	**v** a sea mile	______________

Proofreading

1 Rewrite the following misspelt words correctly.

a politican ______________ **b** neccesary ______________

c feasable ______________ **d** truge ______________

2 Add any missing punctuation.

It was Dr Jonas Salk who invented the first polio vaccine And who was Dr Salk He was one of the twentieth century's great medical scientists, along with Drs fleming and florey whose work with penicillin gave the world antibiotics to fight bacterial disease

Idiom

Explain:

1 He didn't have a a leg to stand on in the argument. ______________

____

2 Well, aren't you a little Miss Sunshine! ______________

____

Writing paragraphs and whole texts

1 In the style of advertisement A (first text in chapter) write and lay out an advertisement for a package ski holiday in the Snowy Mountains. Include a rhetorical question as the persuasive factor in your advertisement. The following facts may assist you.

- Package = 3 days and 4 nights accommodation + breakfasts—$180 per person, twin-share.
- Package is available at Murphy's Chalets, Thredbo, Blue Cow and Smiggin Holes for month of July only.
- Bookings are available through Murphy's Snow Hire, 34 George Street, Sydney (ph. 02 9765 9545).
- Discount ski and snow wear hire are available to package purchasers booking before 15 May.

____

____

____

____

____

____

Rewrite the details of this small advertisement in a style and layout that would suggest the mystery and romance of this part of the world. Your text should be in full sentences and refer to the history and architecture of the region.

Middle East Tours

Lebanon & Syria	Jordan & Egypt
Depart 26 April for 17 days $4100	Depart 9 April for 16 days $3900
Tel: 04 7605 3981	email: mide@sa.net.au

3 Draw up your own advertisement for a caravan park by the sea. Your target market is families seeking a Christmas holiday vacation. Your advertisement cannot be expensive, so it will have to be concise and small and its text will have to be written in phrases, not sentences.

Chapter test

1 Join these two sentences with a relative pronoun.

The store sells surf gear. The store is having a sale.

2 Does this sentence make sense? Yes/No

The boy is running late for school with his dog who had a late night.

3 Is this sentence correctly punctuated? Yes/No

Mr Hill wanted to know why I missed swimming practice this morning?

4 Add the correct end punctuation to this sentence. Yes/No

He looked up in alarm, glimpsed flames down the hallway and shouted, Fire

CHAPTER 5

Script

STRUCTURE

title and section detail

cast of characters and costume direction

set/stage directions

introduction

actor directions

rising action—things begin to happen and then came together, e.g.

- *personalities become clear*
- *personality clashes develop*
- *issues are defined*

climax

conclusion: clash between Jack and Ralph averted temporarily

The Sound of the Shell (Act 1)

(based on an incident from the novel, *Lord of the Flies* by William Golding)

Characters:	Ralph	Eric	The boys range in age from 8 to 14.
	Piggy	Johnny	Jack, Ralph and Piggy are the oldest.
	Simon	Roger	They are dressed in the tattered and
	Jack	Henry	water-stained remains of English public
	Sam	Several choir boys	school dress. Piggy is wearing glasses.

Scene opens in a clearing on a tropical island. Ralph and Piggy are present. Ralph is holding a large conch which he blows three times.

Piggy: (*Pointing*) See! I said they'd come! There's one!
(Small boy wanders onto set through brushwood.)
Piggy: (*Importantly*) We better take names, Ralph. I'll do it. <u>What's yer name</u>?
Johnny: Johnny.
(More boys enter including Sam and Eric)
Piggy: Who're you?
Sam: I'm Sam.
Eric: 'n I'm Eric.
Sam + Eric: We're twins.
Piggy: Right. Sam, Eric ... Sam, Eric ...
Eric: (*Laughing*) No, I'm Eric...
Sam: 'n I'm Sam.
(Boys laugh, then silence falls. All eyes turn to Ralph.)
Ralph: We should have a meeting now we're all here ...
(Enter Jack with a column of choristers.)
Jack: (*Imperiously*) <u>Where's the man with the trumpet</u>?
Ralph: <u>There's no man with a trumpet, only me.</u>
Jack: Isn't there a ship, then?
Ralph: No, there isn't anyone, but us. We're having a meeting. Come and join in.
Jack: (*To choir*) Choir! <u>Sta-and still</u>!
Some choir boys: (*Faintly*) But, Merridew. Please, Merridew ... can't we just ...?
(Simon faints, falls out of line.)
Jack: All right, then. Sit down. Let him alone.
Choir boy: But Merridew ...
Jack: You know he's always <u>throwing a faint</u>. He did it in Gibraltar and Addis and ...
(Choir boys snigger.)
Jack: (*to Ralph*) <u>Aren't there any adults</u>?
Ralph: <u>No, just us</u>.
Jack: Then we'll have to take care of ourselves.
Piggy: (*Timidly*) That's why Ralph made a meeting. So as we can decide what to do. We've heard names, from before you were here. That's Johnny. An' those two—they're twins, Sam'n Eric. That's Eric ... you? No, you're Sam <u>... no ...</u>
Ralph: We should all have names. I'm Ralph.
Jack: (*Snorts*) Kids' names! Why should I be Jack? I'm Merridew.
Ralph: But it would be better ...
Piggy: (*Still talking*) Then, that boy ... that's ... I forget ...
Jack: You're talking too much. Shut up, Fatty!
(Laughter)
Ralph: (*Gleefully*) No, he's not Fatty, he's Piggy!
Roger: Piggy!
Jack: (*Laughing*) Oh, Piggy!
(Storm of laughter from all except Piggy.)
Jack: We've got to do something about being rescued.
Henry: (*Tugging Ralph's sleeve*) This isn't fun any more. Can I go home now, please?
Ralph: (*Absently*) Shut up. Seems to me we ought to have a chief to decide things properly.
Small boys: A chief! A chief! Like the Indians!
Jack: (*Arrogantly*) I ought to be chief because I'm chapter chorister and head boy. <u>I can sing C sharp</u>.
(Buzz from boys.)
Jack: Well, that's all right, then.
Roger: Let's have a vote, like an election!
Various boys: Yes! Vote for chief! Let's vote now!
Ralph: But who shall we vote for?
Choir boy: Him with the shell!
Other boys: Ralph! Ralph! Let him be chief with that trumpet thing.
(Ralph raises his hand for silence.)
Ralph: Is there anyone else who wants to be chief. All right, then. Who wants Jack for chief?
(Choir <u>drearily</u> raise their hands.)
Ralph: Who wants me?
(All other hands shoot up, Piggy's grudgingly.)
Ralph: One, two, three, four, five ... (mutter), twelve, thirteen. I'm chief then.
(Applause. Jack flushes.)
Ralph: *(appeasingly)* The choir belongs to you, of course ...

Angeline Baker

LANGUAGE FEATURES

dialogue:

- *identifies personalities*
- *explains background*
- *explains issues*

therefore language:

- *must be precise*
- *can be colloquial*
- *may lack formal structure*

accurate reproduction of small boy's language

two potential leaders speak in complete sentences

military-style speech indicates what sort of person Jack is

colloquialism

simple question and answer defines the issue of the scene

dots indicate pauses in speech

absurd contrast of Jack's qualifications shows his unsuitability for leadership

precise adverb tells how choir really think of Jack

Comprehension

1 A conch is a trumpet. Is this true or false? ____________________

2 Two boys emerge as potential leaders. Who are they?
____________________ and ____________________

3 Underline the correct answer. The boys are:
a camping out **b** alone on an island **c** on a pioneering course

4 Underline the correct answer. Jack's dismissal of Simon's fainting is:
a reasonable **b** callous **c** vindictive **d** punitive

5 Underline the correct answer. The word *imperiously* suggests that Jack is:
a a boss **b** grandly dressed **c** wearing a uniform **d** a leader

6 From your understanding of the personalities in this scene underline which of the following would be the most likely development as the play progresses.
a Sam and Eric become resourceful individuals. **b** Piggy causes trouble.
c A struggle for leadership develops between Jack and Ralph.
d Jack and Ralph develop a cooperative style of dual leadership.

7 Was the election a fair and democratic election? Give reasons for your opinion.

____

____

____

Writing skills

1 List these elements of a script in the order in which they occur in a play.
a stage directions **b** scene and set directions **c** cast of characters

____

2 Setting and stage directions must be brief. How many facts are contained in the three sentences this script devotes to them? ____________________

3 Underline the correct alternative. The direction (*Importantly*) in Piggy's second line is meant to guide the actor's voice production/movement.

4 Insert the missing letters. The technique of having the boys identify themselves to each other also introduces them to the a _ _ _ _ _ _ e.

5 Which line clearly tells us Jack believes he is more grown-up than the others?

____

6 Insert the missing letters and word. We learn as much about a character from the re _ c t _ _ n of other characters to him as we do from his own words and actions. We know Jack is a boss because of the choir boys' ____________________ to his standing for election as chief.

7 Underline the most precise answer. The writer wants us to know from the line *I can sing C sharp* that Jack:
a can sing that note **b** is a potential leader
c is arrogant **d** is rather silly in his self-importance

8 The conch serves two purposes in this script. Underline the two purposes.

a a narrative purpose **b** a symbolic purpose **c** a humorous purpose **d** a costume purpose

9 Underline which two of the following best describe the dialogue of this script.

a colloquial **b** vague **c** obscure **d** age appropriate

10 Insert the missing letters and words. All plays deal with (i) things that happen and (ii) ideas that are controversial. We call these inc _ d _ _ ts and iss _ _ s. In this scene the meeting is the ______________________ and the need for leadership among people is the ______________________.

11 The humour to engage audience interest early comes from the small boys. Why do you think do they were given the humorous exchange and not any of the older boys?

____

____

____

Vocabulary

conflict	**characterisation**	**issue**	**incident**	**character**
analyse	**consider**	**assess**	**discuss**	**argue**

You will use each of these words many times in your English course. Learn how to spell and use them thoroughly now. The terms in the top row are used when talking about drama. The terms in the bottom row are all ways of talking about issues in a play.

Focus on punctuation

Dialogue

- The exact words spoken by someone are always enclosed in inverted commas (except in a drama script where it would be absurd), e.g.
  'Will you take the role of Banquo's ghost?' the director asked John.
- If more than one person is speaking, begin a new paragraph each time the speaker changes, e.g.
  'Aren't I too tall for a ghost?' asked John.
  'Of course not,' laughed the director. 'Ghosts can be tall, short, fat or thin.'

Note: You may use single or double inverted commas to indicate dialogue. Single inverted commas are used in this book.

1 Put inverted commas where needed.

a The centre light is not focused! the director shouted.

b Where is my sword? wailed the boy playing Hamlet.

c Macbeth famously asked, Is this a dagger which I see before me?

d The fog machine put out so much fog that actors were calling, Where are you? I can't see you!

2 Punctuate the following dialogue using [to indicate the start of a new paragraph.

Do you ever have nightmares? Peter asked his brother. Not any more. I used to have them when I was little. What sort of things did you dream about, David? Oh, getting lost, falling down holes, that sort of thing. What are your nightmares about, Petey? Getting thumped up by Skink. Who's Skink? Is he that kid in Year 10 with the red hair? Yeah, that's him. Look, Petey, if he's bothering you, you tell me and I'll sort it out. No one's bullying my little brother.

Select a word

Change these verbs to nouns and then to adjectives using suffixes (endings such as *~tion*, *~ment*, *~able*, *~ive*, etc.)

1 argue ____________________ ____________________

2 analyse ____________________ ____________________

3 discuss ____________________ ____________________

4 consider ____________________ ____________________

Grammar

Verbs

- **Verbs** do things or are things, e.g.
  Eat your dinner, you are slower than a snail eating lettuce today.
- Verbs come in different forms:
  - the **infinitive** (the basic form from which all verb parts are made), e.g.
    to run, to cry, to laugh
  - **finite verbs** (complete verbs with one or more parts), e.g.
    walk, will walk, was walking, am walking etc.
- Finite verbs often include helping parts called **helping verbs**, e.g.
  Lucy had missed the train.
- Always be careful that the helping verb is in the same tense as the rest of the sentence, e.g.
  The theatre company has disbanded tomorrow. INCORRECT
  The theatre company will disband tomorrow. CORRECT
- Generally, infinitives should not be split, e.g.
  He wanted to quickly read the book. INCORRECT
  He wanted to read the book quickly. CORRECT

1 Underline the infinitives and circle the finite verbs.

a Our class went to see the Bell Shakespeare Company's production of *Hamlet*.

b To see a live production of any play is a thrilling experience.

2 Write 'finite verb', 'helping verb' or 'infinitive' to name the underlined verbs.

a Charles has managed the theatre lighting for the past five years. ____________

b Alisha is thrilled to have been chosen to play the lead role. ____________

c To make a career of costume drama is Miley's ambition. ____________

d Ryan has been practising his lines all day. ____________

e Josh was selected because he was the right build for that character. ____________

3 Underline the helping verbs.

a was starring **b** was staged **c** had cast **d** will design

e were producing **f** are rehearsing **g** is directing **h** am auditioning

4 Insert an appropriate form of the verb indicated in the following.

a Stephen Spielberg ______ ____________________ (know) for spectacular special effects.

b Stars on TV soaps all want ______ ____________________ (play) a great dramatic role.

c Pop groups that are successful ______ usually __________________ (produce) an excellent video clip.

d The Bangarra Dance Theatre ______ well ____________________ (receive) on its recent international tour.

5 Rewrite the following correctly.

a She needs to correctly rewrite that letter. ____________________

b To continually practise is the way to improve. ____________________

c She and I is going to the Easter Show. ____________________

d Michael acting the part of King Lear. ____________________

e The play is opening yesterday. ____________________

Word study

1 Complete using words from the top row of the vocabulary list.

a You go to bed at 10 pm. Your parents say that is too late. You disagree. This is a ____________.

b In this situation the ____________ at the heart of the conflict is: what is a suitable bedtime?

c Some television shows depend on violent ____________s for the action in their scripts.

d The ____________ of the hero in a novel must be fully developed..

e The ____________ of the inhabitants of South Park is particularly unpleasant.

2 Match words from the bottom row of the vocabulary list to these meanings.

a to talk about ____________

b to examine each component part ____________

c to think about ____________

d to weigh up the value of something ____________

e to take a different point of view ____________

3 Write an appropriate word from the top row in each space.

a When we ________ these rainfall figures, we can see a drought pattern emerging.

b The insurer came to ________ the damage to his car, but Mr Jones was not at home.

c It's rather nice to sit in the sun and ________ the weekend football.

d Would you ________ going with me to see a film this afternoon?

e Those twins are so quarrelsome they would ________ over whether it was raining or not.

Evaluating other people's writing

Craig: Don't come in. Can't you read? The sign says 'Go away'.
Sally: Well, it's a stupid sign. It should say 'No trespassers'.
Craig: What does that mean?
Sally: It tells people to go away.
Craig: That's what my sign says.
Sally: But it's a stupid sign. No one puts stuff like that on a sign.

1 Underline the missing elements of this script.

a dialogue b scene setting c cast of characters d title e stage directions

2 Underline the correct answer.

a The issue is:
i permission to enter
ii Sally's rudeness

b The incident is:
i Sally's attempted entry
ii the argument about Sally's entry

Word usage

1 *Can* is used when something is possible and *may* is used when something is *allowed*, e.g.

*You **may** go fishing if you **can** find some bait.*
(may = are allowed to; can = are able to)

Insert *can* and *may* as appropriate.

a Rowan ____________________ play the tuba like a virtuoso.

b Claudia ____________________ audition for Lady Macbeth's part if she ____________________ guarantee to attend rehearsals.

c After you shut down the lighting system you ____________________ leave.

d We ____________________ give you a lift to the opening night.

e ____________________ I eat that last lamington?

2 The verb *differ* and the adjective *different* are followed by *from*, e.g.

eggs differ from apples in shape. CORRECT

eggs are different to apples in shape. INCORRECT

Eggs are different from apples in shape. CORRECT

Eggs are different than apples in shape. INCORRECT

Insert *from* or *to* as appropriate.

a The twins differ ____________________ each other in height.

b Cats are very different ____________________ dogs.

c City life differs markedly ____________________ rural life.

d Olivier's Hamlet is a very different character ____________________ Kenneth Branagh's.

3 Make any necessary corrections. (Not all are incorrect.)

a Can we join you for coffee after the show? ____________________

b Luhrmann's *Romeo and Juliet* is different than Zeffirelli's. ____________________

c If the star is ill, we can see her understudy perform tonight. ____________________

d If you are prepared to learn your lines, you may audition for a part. ____________________

Quick think

1 *luna* = moon (Latin)

a A *lunar* month is the same as a calendar month. Is this true or false? ____________________

b A *lunar* module is a spacecraft in orbit around the moon. Is this true or false? ____________________

c Insert the missing letters. Long ago people believed madness to be caused by the phases of the moon, hence the word l _ _ _ tic.

2 *tele* = far off (Greek). Insert the misssing letters.

a an instrument for distance vision	tele _ _ _ _ e
b selling products over the phone	tele _ _ _ _ _ _ _ _ _ g
c a live show filmed for television	tele _ _ _ t
d transmission of thought between people	tele _ _ _ _ y
e supposed ghostly movement of distant objects	tele _ _ _ _ _ is

3 *geo* = concerning the earth (Greek). Write *geo~* words to match these meanings.

a Study of the earth's strata and the rocks and minerals found there	geo _ _ _ _
b Study of the world's landforms and the way of life lived on them	geo _ _ _ _ _ _
c Energy produced by boiling geysers and mud springs	geo _ _ _ _ _ _ _ energy

Proofreading

1 Rewrite correctly:

a ordition ______________________ **b** insident ______________________

c isshue ______________________ **d** reahersal ______________________

e argew ______________________ **f** dialoge ______________________

2 Correct the punctuation. (Don't forget paragraphs.)

What did J.M. Barrie write asked a student. *Peter Pan* came the reply. I thought that was a film. Yes it was, but it was a stage play before it was made into a film. I have a copy of the script you may read it if you like.

Idiom

Explain:

1 Don't waste your breath. He's not listening. ______________________

____

2 I just can't get my head around algebra. ______________________

____

Writing paragraphs and whole texts

1 Write the scene setting for a bus stop meeting between a boy and a girl from different high schools on a wet afternoon. Locate one of the students in the setting. Make sure that someone reading your directions will have enough information to create on stage the scene you have in your mind. Include details about the time of day; presence of other people; bus shelter's appearance and location; surrounding buildings, etc. Use your own paper.

2 Assume the boy in this bus stop scene is painfully shy. Write a 10-line dialogue for the two students from the early part of their conversation at the bus stop. (Don't forget directions for voice delivery and actor movement.) Use your own paper.

Chapter test

1 Circle the word spelt incorrectly.

a characterisation **b** assess **c** anylise **d** argue

2 Which sentence is correct?

a Solly and his mates playing cricket yesterday. **b** Solly and his mates were playing cricket yesterday.

3 Which sentence is correct?

a The green team's goalie have shot three baskets before half time.

b The green team's goalie has shot three baskets before half time.

4 Which sentence is correctly punctuated?

a Who goes there, cried the nightwatchman

b Who goes there? cried the nightwatchman.

c 'Who goes there?' cried the nightwatchman.

CHAPTER 6

Cartoon

STRUCTURE

all single-frame social comment cartoons

A
balloon text—explains illustration; illustration is linear, contrasted (size, position, dress); it represents major social problem (poor conditions of people producing goods at home for outside business)

B
linear illustration incorporating text; text reverses usual idea of man in charge to comment on computer age

C
detailed, shaded illustration incorporating text; text, an email address, carries weight of message —man searches for meaning in life, but can't escape computerisation of life

Cartoon A

The *Sydney Morning Herald*

Cartoon B

The *Bulletin*

Cartoon C

The *Bulletin*

LANGUAGE FEATURES

language
- *is brief*
- *is succinct*
- *plays on word meaning and context*

A
- *'buzz' implies selfish fun and excitement*
- *'fashion parades' contrasts with slaving over sewing machine*
- *tone of fashionable text: excited tone of working text: factual and flat*
- *deliberate contrasting of 'buzz' and $2 makes the point of the cartoon*

B
- *text is sharp, confident and humorous*
- *contrasts with worried confusion of men*
- *'Heh! Heh' effectively conveys malice*

C
- *flat, soulless text in a sensitively drawn landscape makes point of the cartoon*
- *clever use of email text says it all very accurately and very succinctly*

Comprehension

1 Underline the correct answer. These three cartoons fall into the category of:

a humour **b** social comment **c** slapstick **d** instruction

2 Underline the correct answer. Kaz Cooke in Cartoon A is angry about:

a unthinking society ladies **b** quality of workmanship
c social injustice **d** child labour

3 What is the seated woman doing in Cartoon A? ________________________________

4 Underline the correct answer. Cartoons B and C both deal with:

a computers **b** confused people **c** computer domination of society **d** machines

5 Underline the correct answer. Cartoon B suggests computers:

a communicate **b** can think **c** dominate people **d** are subservient to people

6 Underline the correct answer. Cartoon C is meant to make you:

a think **b** laugh **c** grow superstitious **d** email God

Writing skills

1 Insert the missing letters. The contrast in Cartoon A is expressed in ill _ _ _ _ _ tion and in t _ _ t.

2 Insert these two underlined phrases appropriately in the following statement.

a whim and harsh reality

In Cartoon A the top statement is an expression of **a** ____________________ and the bottom statement is an expression of **b** ____________________.

3 Which word in the top statement (in Cartoon A) tells us that this woman does not have to worry about the serious things in life, only its pleasures? ____________________

4 Which statement (top or bottom) in Cartoon A carries the **punchline** (point of the cartoon)? ______________

5 What visual item in Cartoon A explains the connection between the two women?

____

6 Name three things in Cartoon A that visually demonstrate the contrast between the two women.

______________________ ______________________ ______________________

7 How does the cartoonist suggest the machinist has been working for many hours?

____

8 Insert one of these terms in the following statement.

moods, abilities, decision-making, activities

Cartoon B works visually by contrasting the ____________________ of people and computers.

9 Underline the alternative that does not apply. The text of Cartoon B suggests that computers are:

a smug **b** arrogant **c** confident **d** intellectual

10 Underline the correct answer. The cartoonist has used *Heh! Heh*! and not *Ha! Ha!* or *Ho! Ho!* to convey a suggestion of:

a malice **b** inferiority **c** jollity **d** boredom

11 These three cartoons each tell us about some aspect of our society. The mood of each is different. Match the mood to the cartoon.

A —	**i**	angry
B —	**ii**	forlorn
C —	**iii**	acidly critical (satirical)

Vocabulary

visual	**stark**	**linear**	**meticulous**	**bold**
photograph	**graphic**	**caricature**	**illustration**	**depiction**

The terms in the top row are adjectives that describe the way a cartoon is drawn. For example, Somerville draws with *meticulous* detail and Kaz Cooke's illustrations are *boldly* drawn. The terms in the bottom row are nouns referring to the kind of picture that can be included in a cartoon. Underline the 'ph' in *graphic* and *photograph*. This is a common spelling pattern. Then learn all the words using the Look, Cover, Write, Check method, being careful with *meticulous* and *caricature*, which sometimes cause trouble.

Focus on punctuation

Commas

- **Commas** separate lists of things or activities, e.g.
  Tanya plays netball, hockey, tennis and cricket.

Note: *and* takes the place of a comma between the last two items in a list.

- **Commas** separate nouns from their explanation, e.g.
  Tony Lockett, legendary goal kicker for the Swans, retired in 1999.

1 Insert commas where necessary.

a David the identical twin of Duncan equalled their elder brother's 100 m record.

b Mr Jones who always wears red socks is our maths teacher.

c The men of the Kokoda Trail swam rivers climbed mountains cut their way through jungle and halted the enemy advance.

d He stowed bread cheese dried fruit and water in his backpack.

e In this park dogs skateboards and bicycles are prohibited.

2 Insert commas where necessary.

a He was looking for his best friend a black-and-tan kelpie dog.

b King parrots large birds with tomato red and emerald plumage are mountain parrots.

c Joseph an unusually talented musician can play both the flute and the bassoon.

d The land east of the Blue Mountains the land first settled by Europeans was land belonging to the Eora Tharawal and Dharrug peoples.

Select a word

Using the Greek word *photos* (light) as a base, write words that mean:

1 a copying machine ____________

2 always looks good in photographs ____________

3 a close race finish ____________

4 abnormal fear of light ____________

5 news in photographs ____________

6 one who takes photographs ____________

Grammar

Verb forms—present participles

- A **finite verb** with more than one part contains a helping verb and a participle.
- In **continuous tenses** finite verbs contain **present participles** (verb forms ending in *~ing*), e.g. *Mr Sung is visiting relatives in Hong Kong.*
  Auxiliary Present participle
- Helping verbs include *have, has, had, was, were, am, is, are, will, shall.*

1 Underline the present participles in the following:

a Someone said you are intending to become a cartoonist.

b Kaz Cooke is criticising the harsh system of outsourcing clothing manufacture.

c Larson's most famous cartoons show cows who are behaving like people.

d Cartoon characters are now starring in full-length films.

e The *Happy Feet* penguins are dancing their way into more films.

2 Insert the correct verb form in the following sentences, which are all in the present continuous tense.

a Grim grey clouds ______________________________ (gather) on the horizon.

b A southern right whale ______________________________ (frolic) in Sydney Harbour.

c The victims of the recent earthquakes _______ still ________________________ (relive) the nightmare.

d Racehorses _________________ (train) on the beach at sunrise today.

e Proud owners _________________ (exhibit) their vintage cars in the park this week.

Word study

1 Match these meanings to words from the vocabulary list.

a exaggerated comic drawing of a person ____________________________

b computer-generated diagram/chart/graph ____________________________

c picture accompanying a piece of text ____________________________

d picture formed by light on film ____________________________

2 Match an appropriate word from the vocabulary list to these cartoon characteristics.

a detailed ________________________

b drawn in dramatic black lines ________________________

c drawn without shading ________________________

d a representation ________________________ or ________________________

3 Are the following true or false?

a The sound of a waterfall is a *visual* effect. ________________________

b A cartoon with a single sheep skeleton in the middle of a bare paddock would be a *stark* depiction of drought. ________________________

c A pattern of circles is a linear drawing. ______________

d A meticulous person keeps haphazard records. __________

4 Complete these sentences with a word from the list.

a A political cartoon would present a politician as a _____________ of him or herself.

b In a children's book an _______________ is as important as the text of the story.

c I have a black and white ___________________ of my great-grandparents.

d Thick black lines always make a _ _ _ _ statement in a cartoon.

5 All of these words contain the 'ph' spelling. Can you complete them?

- **a** paper lined in grid fashion g _ _ _ _ paper
- **b** a chemical that burns with a cold blue light _ _ os _ _ _ _ us
- **c** a mythical bird that rises again from its own ashes _ _ _ enix
- **d** one who things about the great issues of life _ _ ilos _ _ _ er
- **e** fear of open spaces a _ _ r _ _ _ obia

Word usage

1 Cartoons are often concerned with current affairs. These two cartoons from 1999 both deal with an issue that arose concerning the Sydney 2000 Olympics. For a while it looked as if people who had already bought their tickets might not be able to see the event that they had paid to see because events had been rescheduled. (This problem was later satisfactorily resolved.)

Cartoon A

Cartoon B

The *Sydney Morning Herald*

- **a** Which cartoon has the most direct text on the issue? ____________________
- **b** To crystallise the idea of people's choice what name do both cartoonists use? ____________________
- **c** Underline all the correct answers. This name was used because:
  - **i** it is a high profile name
  - **ii** this is an exceptional athlete
  - **iii** it is as good as any other name to use
  - **iv** it is easily recognised
  - **v** it fitted the space available
  - **vi** Australians identify with her
- **d** Insert the missing letters. Cartoon A employs the technique of offering small c _ m f _ _ t to the spectator who does not see Freeman run.
- **e** Underline the correct alternative. Both cartoons approve/disapprove of the rescheduling of events after ticket sales closed.
- **f** Underline the correct answer. The purpose of these current issue cartoons is mainly to:
  - **i** make people laugh
  - **ii** make people think

2 **Redundant words** are unnecessary or repetitious words. Redundancy spoils good writing, e.g. *Pens are unnecessary and not needed in this exam.*

- **a** Underline the redundant words.
  - **i** The lofty high mountain reached into the clouds.
  - **ii** Floodwaters turned the plain into a gigantic, enormous lake.
  - **iii** Duck Creek used to be a murky, discoloured, stinking, foul-smelling stream.
- **b** Replace the underlined words with a single noun.
  - **i** Old Mr Ho was a person who used to build ships in Singapore. ____________________
  - **ii** Mrs Townsend is a person trained to counsel those who experience grief or trauma. ____________________
  - **iii** Cliff Small is a person who arbitrates disputes between players at football matches. ____________________

c Find a single verb to complete the rewriting of the following.

i Don't change your mind and break this agreement.
Don't r _ n _ g _ on this agreement.

ii Mrs Williams can give you authority to do this.
Mrs Williams can a _ _ _ _ _ ise you to do this.

iii To receive and register the new Year 7 students will take several hours.
To e _ _ _ _ the new Year 7 students will take several hours.

d Shorten by removing redundancies and by replacing phrases with single words wherever possible.

The old man, who was a fisherman from Budgewoi, fishing on the bank at the edge of the river caught nothing all day and went home empty-handed without any fish.

Quick think

1 Insert the missing letters to show what is emphasised in a caricature.

a distinctive parts of the face — f _ c _ _ l f _ _ t _ _ _ s
b distinctive walk — g _ _ t
c distinctive habits — m _ n _ _ r _ _ ms
d distinctive hand movements — g _ _ t _ r _ s

2 Match these cartooning techniques with their explanation.

a	cross-hatching	**i**	speech text in a circle over the head of its speaker
b	shading	**ii**	diagonally meshed lines to give substance to a drawing
c	speech balloon	**iii**	small item that appears in every work of a cartoonist
d	signature item	**iv**	variations of light and dark giving depth to a cartoon

3 Insert the missing letters to complete these principles of cartoon text-writing.

a Use few words. Be b _ _ _ f.
b Be exact. Be pr _ c _ se.
c Compress a lot of meaning into a few words. Be c _ m p _ ct.
d Make text and illustration work together. Text and illustrations should c _ _ pl _ m _ _ t each other.

Proofreading

Correct all punctuation.

We all live in a yellow submarine sang my father rather tunelessly I thought my mother broke in with a snatch from Eleanor Rigby about all the lonely people but it was when my elder brother whom I'd always thought sensible began banging two tins together and bellowing Penny Lane that I knew my family was seriously deranged old-fashioned Beatlemania had them in its grasp.

Idiom

Explain:

1 He only lives a stone's throw from me. ____________________

____

2 He doesn't have a leg to stand on in that debate. ____________________

____

Writing paragraphs and whole texts

1 Larson, the famous American cartoonist, often draws animals doing things humans would do to create cartoons that make people laugh at how absurd we humans can be. The following are two captions he has used in such cartoons. Draw a cartoon (using an animal) to suit each caption and touch people's sense of the ridiculous.

a Get it off me! Get it off me!

b 'I just gotta be me ...'

2 Write captions for these.

a

b

3 Draw a cartoon with text that suggests road rage is juvenile behaviour. Use both 'balloon' text and caption text, with 'baby talk' in the balloon and formal English in the caption.

Chapter test

1 Is *meticulous* correctly used in this sentence? Yes/No

Scott's handwriting is <u>meticulous</u>, all over the place and full of crossings out.

2 Circle the correct word.

I enjoy hearing a magpie warble. It is a lovely visual/auditory experience.

3 Mark ✗ where commas are missing in this sentence.

That man the one with the feather in his hat does not look very well.

4 Is this sentence correctly punctuated? Yes/No

The Wilsons planned a summer holiday of swimming, boating, fishing, and just lying around on the beach.

CHAPTER 7

Poem

STRUCTURE

purpose: to enable reader to share an experience of the poet through all his senses and mind

title: gives clue to poet's emphasis in talking about the subject (storm); emphasis is on how people react to such a display of nature's power

introduction

verses 1 and 2 tell us about what the boy and his dog do while the storm approaches

development

climax

verse 3
the storm

conclusion

verse 4
places boy in the context of his adult family; then returns to first image of little boy alone with his dog out on an adventure

Storm over Woolloomooloo

With his grey umbrella
he is holding up the sky, stopping rain
from falling over the city—
the little boy in red clothes
walking barefoot on tiptoes:
followed by a dog
at the edge of the city.

Oblivious of storms or danger
he leads his dog
across the gaze of the Domain, the rising
stare of Kings Cross
and the wayside presence of terraces—
his dog with a patch
over one eye:
that follows him obediently
into the weather.

A foreground of spreading greens and blue
cannot dispel the darkness
of gathering clouds—
the present caught up with the future
in a downpour of rain and thunder.

In the meantime he slips out
and braves the elements,
away from grown-ups and cautioning voices—
in the company of his dog
he crosses the Domain
and like an apparition he quickly vanishes.

Feter Skrzynecki
(From *Easter Sunday*, HarperCollins, Sydney)

LANGUAGE FEATURES

strong visual images
simple language—very condensed

image of power (a metaphor) (little boy defies storm)

contrast (little boy versus whole sky)

metaphor for all the windows of Kings Cross buildings on hill

clear visual images—concise (e.g. 'wayside', 'terraces', 'patch')

condensed description (sea, trees, grass)

very condensed description of waiting as storm develops and then experiencing storm

return to first idea of power

return to first verse image

abrupt disappearance that suggests: did poet see the boy or just imagine him?

Comprehension

1 Underline the correct statement in reference to the poem.

a It is raining **b** It is threatening to rain.

2 Find three words in the poem that locate this incident in Sydney.

________________ ________________ ________________

3 Insert the missing words. We learn that the little boy is wearing ________________, is ________________, holds an ________________ and has a ________________ for a companion.

4 The little boy has no concern or thought about the weather. Is this true or false? ____________________

5 Underline the correct answer. *A foreground of spreading greens and blue* refers to:

a grass and sky **b** grass, trees and sky **c** grass, trees and sea

6 What do you understand by the words *the present caught up with the future*? Think about the weather and the sky before you answer. ____________________

____

7 What might the *cautioning voices* be saying? ____________________

8 What are the elements referred to in the words *he slips out / and braves the elements*?

____

9 Underline the correct word. An *apparition* is:

a a person **b** a ghost **c** a stranger

Writing skills

1 *He is holding up the sky.* Is this **literal** (true fact) language or **figurative** (imaginative) language?

____

2 Underline the correct alternative. That image (picture) referred to in question 1 shows us the dominance/insignificance of the little boy in the landscape.

3 What word in the second verse tells us the little boy is unaware of storms or danger? ____________________

4 What words suggest that the dog trusts the boy? ____________________

5 What two words suggest that the city is watching the little boy and his dog as they walk?

____________________ ____________________

6 In verse 3 the boy is walking in the present. What lines describe the present?

____

7 The future is also described in this verse. What lines refer to the future?

____

8 What words bring the two ideas of present and future together as one image?

____

The last verse returns to the idea of the boy's being small and slight. What verb suggests this?

____________________ What noun emphasises it? ____________________

10 Insert the missing letters. This slightness is contrasted with the power of the el _ _ _ _ ts, and the verb 'b _ _ _ _ s' tells us the poet has been moved by the sight of one little boy challenging their power.

11 Underline the correct answer. This poem:

a simply tells a story **b** describes a boy and his dog

c is about the poet's being moved by the sight of a very little human being defying the power of nature.

12 Underline which of the following techniques the poet has employed.

a visual imagery **b** alliteration **c** incidental (occasional) rhyme **d** onomatopoeia **e** simile

Vocabulary

coarse	**livid**	**harsh**	**sinuous**	**pungent**
flecked	**scented**	**doughy**	**shimmering**	**fluid**

Our five senses are sight, hearing, touch, smell and taste. Poets appeal to our senses when they write so we can share what they are experiencing. All the words in the vocabulary list are useful adjectives to use when we try to describe what our senses know. Learn to spell and use them correctly.

Note: the 'sc' spelling of *scented*. Other words using this 'sc' spelling include: *scene, sceptre, science* and *scimitar*.

Focus on punctuation

Colons

Colons separate a statement from its listed clarification e.g.

The information was of interest to those in attendance: the principal, the deputy, the teachers and the parents.
The students stated their causes of discontent: crowded classes, inadequate resources and an inflexible timetable.

Colons can also mark the beginning of a quotation, e.g.

As the poet Laurence Binyon wrote: 'Lest we forget.'

Punctuate the following.

1. The hard men of eighties cinema are now all old men Steve McQueen Clint Eastwood Sylvester Stallone and Arnold Schwarzenegger.
2. Skimming through the plays of Shakespeare she came across Lady Macbeth's famous line 'All the perfumes of Arabia will not sweeten this little hand.'
3. The causes of the Eureka rebellion were varied resentment of the gold licence fee police brutality and the provocative conduct of the government.
4. The Valley of the Kings has revealed unbelievable treasures mummies of ancient pharaohs gold caskets gold death masks and gold funerary gifts.
5. One of John O'Brien's most quoted lines about drought and flood is We'll all be rooned, said Hanrahan.

Select a word

Choose the <u>best</u> word from the list below to describe the following.

ring, scratchy, gritty, chime, clang, toll, sticky, clammy

1. the sound of a pendulum clock telling the hour ____________________
2. the sound of a very large and heavy bell ____________________
3. the feel of sand in the eye ____________________
4. the touch of a cold, damp hand ____________________

Grammar

Past participles

- Finite verbs of more than one part used in the past tense always include a helping verb and a **past participle**, e.g.
  Alanah has finished her homework.
  Auxiliary Past participle
- Past participles very often end in *~ed* as in *finished* in the example above, but many do not, e.g.
  Mark has bought ice-creams for all of us.
  Some common past participles that do not end in *~ed* are: *seen, brought, caught, gone, come, swum, ridden, taught, flown, seen, rung, eaten, drunk, bought*
- Be careful with past participles that look similar and with simple past tense verbs that look like past participles, e.g.
  bought (from to buy) and *brought* (from to bring); *hung* (from *to hang a picture*) and *hanged* (from *to hang a person*); *lied* (to lie/tell a lie), *laid* (from *to lay something* somewhere or *to lay a table*) and *lain* (from *to lie down*)

1 Insert an appropriate past participle of your choice.

a They have ______________________ 3000 stamps.

b I ate one ice-cream but Steve has ______________________ seven.

c Our car is at the garage to be ______________________.

d Laura had ______________________ the book before seeing the film.

2 **a** Underline the past participle in these verbs.

i had hurried **ii** has eaten **iii** have gone **iv** were caught

v has ridden **vi** had swum **vii** have drunk **viii** had brought

b Write the past participle of these verbs.

i to chase ______________________ **ii** to dance ______________________

iii to fly ______________________ **iv** to catch ______________________

3 Underline the correct past participles in these sentences.

a He was in gaol because he had lied/laid under oath.

b Mrs Frankel has lain/laid the table.

c Susie has laid/lain asleep for hours.

d Ned Kelly was hung/hanged in Melbourne gaol.

e Pictures of famous Australians are hanged/hung in the National Portrait Gallery.

f Susan brought/bought the latest album to top the charts.

g We were surprised to find Paul had brought/bought his horse to the picnic.

h The valuable old book was carefully laid/lain on the desk.

4 Tick the sentences with correct verbs and cross those with incorrect verbs.

a To our horror Bluey had bought a dead snake into the house. ___

b The exhausted swimmers had all lain down where they crawled out of the pool. ___

c Today I bought a cricket bat and Martin said he had bought one yesterday as well. ___

d A photo of the successful Under Fifteen AFL team was hanged in the school foyer. ___

Word study

Sense response words

1 Find a word from the vocabulary list to describe the following.

a both a poor quality soap and a tone of voice ____________________

b something speckled ____________________

c the light of a mirage ____________________

d an age-whitened scar ____________________

2 Insert a word from the vocabulary list in the following.

a Wire-haired terriers have very ____________________ fur.

b The baker plunged his hands into the ____________________ mixture.

c Green tree snakes hung in ____________________ loops in the branches.

d The ____________________ movement of great athletes makes running seem effortless.

3 Match the words on the left to what they describe on the right.

a	pungent	**i**	someone white in the face with anger
b	scented	**ii**	rough-grained sandpaper
c	livid	**iii**	the smell of rotting fish
d	coarse	**iv**	a rose garden

4 Write an appropriate word beginning with *sc* in each space.

a The ____________ from Sandy's window stretched as far as a blue line of mountains.

b A sword has a straight blade but a ___________ has a curved blade.

c Kings carry a ____________ on official occasions as a sign of royal authority.

d Geology is an earth __________ but microbiology is a medical science.

Word usage

1 Poets use words imaginatively. The following images are all from poems about Sydney by these Australian poets: Jemal Sharah, John Tranter, John Foulcher, Robert Grey, Les Murray, Bruce Beaver, Vivian Smith, Kenneth Slessor and Rosemary Dobson. Can you match the subject and its image?

a	milk bottles	**i**	'the white collapsing foam'
b	a suburban cat	**ii**	'speaking the language of the rain deceitfully'
c	parked cars	**iii**	'the summit that exhilarates cars'
d	doors of slum dwellings	**iv**	'seaweed shuffles on the blurred sand'
e	great surf waves	**v**	'the light of summer with its bone-white glare'
f	summer	**vi**	'the oily aubergine dark of the harbour'
g	a cormorant (shag)	**vii**	'… always snail dribble across the concrete'
h	surf at night	**viii**	'The cat with its back arched to a query'
i	on top of Gladesville bridge	**ix**	'strung together as close as caterpillars'
j	Sydney Harbour at night	**x**	'stretches out its black umbrella wings'
k	water's edge	**xi**	'like shiny black coffin lids'
l	barbecuing sausages	**xii**	'that arched their mackerel backs and smacked the sand'

2

- A **metaphor** is a comparison that is so close that one thing is described as if it were another, e.g.
  The wind prowled and growled *around the house for most of the night.*
  (The metaphor here is one of a predatory animal.)
- Good writers keep their metaphors consistent. Poor writers mix several metaphors together, spoiling the effect of their work, e.g.
  Pete dropped his bundle, threw in the towel *and* cashed in his chips.
  (Three unrelated metaphors make Pete's depression a joke, not a serious problem.)

Write M (metaphor) or MM (mixed metaphor) after each of the following.

a Mr Jones cut a swathe through milling spectators to reach the injured player. ________

b Miss Adams was a new broom in our classroom, a breath of fresh air and just what the doctor ordered. ________

c Carlos was a great bull of a man with an eagle eye and the strength of a lion. ________

d Year 9 marched across the quad, made a quick sortie into the Ag. Plot, retreated, right flanked the main building and finally located their quarry, Year 12, on the basketball courts. There they launched a major assault on the Seniors' refusal to have them on the Snowy excursion. ________

3 Rewrite sentences 2b and 2c to improve them.

a ____

b ____

Quick think

An example of onomatopoeia: *Cats miaow*. Complete the following onomatopoeic words.

1 parrots — sc _ _ _ ch and sq _ _ _ k

2 sparrows — tw _ _ _ _ r

3 flying foxes — squ _ _ l

4 high surf — th _ _ d _ rs

5 a set of keys — cl _ _ ks and j _ _ g _ es

6 a single drop of water into water — pl _ _ s

Proofreading

1 Rewrite misspelt words.

douhy, punjent, shimmering, coarse, livad, sinuwus, fluid

____

2 Correct the punctuation.

Australian teenager Andrew Perrin single-handedly sailed his yacht seaflight around the world in 1997 he was still only seventeen when he rounded Cape horn at the foot of south America where so many ships have come to grief in the past.

3 Check for incorrect verbs and incorrect past participles.

The swagman in the song Waltzing Matilda had stolen a sheep. When the owner had rode up and saw his sheep going to be cooked he bought up the local mounted police to arrest the swagman. However, the swagman was having none of this and jumps into the billabong, never to be seen again. Many people then did not know how to swim so the swagman probably drowned. If he had swam he could have been across the water and away before the troopers catched him.

Idiom

Explain:

1 Take care in your dealilngs with that man. He'll pull a fast one as soon as look at you.

____

2 Craig: I don't know whether I should try squash as a sport—it's very fast.
Fergus: Go on! Take a punt! You'll probably love the game. ______________________

____

Writing paragraphs and whole texts

1 You are on the beach on a summer's day. What do you see? Hear? Smell? Taste? Touch? Feel?

a Make a list of these on the left of the page.

b On the right of the page write as many words as you can that describe what you have listed on the left.

e.g. SAND salty, granular, squeaking, sparkling, chafing

____

____

____

____

____

____

____

____

2 Group the ideas on the left above into three groups of related ideas like this:

damp sand
soldier crab sand mounds
tide limit fan of tiny shells
creeping tide water

} one group idea: the waterline

3 Using each group above as the basis of a verse, write a three-verse poem about a day at the beach in summer. Try to ensure that your reader hears what you hear (use onomatopoeia and alliteration), sees what you see (use vivid images) and feels what you feel (use similes of touch).

Chapter test

1 Which sentence is correct? a __ or b__ ?

a That sheep has course wool.

b That sheep has coarse wool.

2 Which sentence is correctly punctuated? a __ or b __ ?

a All breeds were represented: corgis, terriers, weimaraners, dalmatians, even chihuahuas.

b All breeds were represented corgis, terriers weimaraners dalmatians even chihuahuas.

3 Circle the correct word.

Miley has brought/bought her dog to school.

4 Write the correct past participle of the verb in brackets in the space provided.

He knew he could do it because he had ____________ (to swim) this distance before

Explanation/Instruction

STRUCTURE

purpose: to instruct reader in method of doing something

title

explanatory subtitle

section heading

introduction (handlebar facts)

body of information (what you need)

conclusion (how a good rider uses these)

Smart Set-Ups

Prepare before you ride it—It'll make a difference

GOOD BARS AND BAD BARS

Handlebars or hangers come in various sizes to suit riders of different heights. Bars are described as having various bends and the bend determines the bar's height above the headstock on which it is mounted.

The correct bars for you are those which feel comfortable when you're standing on the pegs, and which don't obstruct your legs when you're sitting well forward on the bike. When adjusted, the bars should give you sufficient space between the bars and the tank. You have to put your leg in this position when cornering and bars adjusted too far forward will cramp your legs.

As well as bars with various bends you can buy bars with different sweep-back angles on the grip. Bars with more sweep-back allow shorter riders to maintain their grip on the bars when they have their weight toward the rear of the bike.

Good riders carry their elbows high to get maximum leverage on the bars. It's very difficult to use this high elbow action if you're using narrow bars. Enduro riders sometimes narrow their bars so they can get through tight terrain more easily, but, in my opinion, if you're riding a 125 or larger bike on a motocross or supercross track you should use 80 cm bars, or bars on which your hands are 80 cm apart. A good way to start with bar position is to adjust the crossbrace so it's parallel to the ground, then make adjustments from there.

Dirt Bike: Tips and Techniques magazine

LANGUAGE FEATURES

biking jargon

informal (conversational) style

simple, factual, direct; no adjectives, no images, just fact

short factual topic sentence

pronoun 'you' makes direct reader contact

persuasive language

racing terms and technical language give impression of authority

precise instruction: brief, pointed, logical

Comprehension

1 Insert the missing word. Handlebars are mounted on a ____________________

2 Underline the correct answer. The height of handlebars is:

a its highest point from the ground **b** the height of its bend above the headstock

c its highest point above the centre line of the frame

3 Underline the correct answer. Sweep-back angles on the grip advantage:

a good riders **b** Enduro riders **c** short riders

4 Insert the missing words. Tight terrain encourages some riders to ______________________________

5 'Tight' terrain means:

a a rocky uneven track
b steep rocky ground
c a course with sharp bends
d a difficult uneven course with tight bends

6 Insert the missing words. Good riders **a** ______________________________ to get

b ______________________________ .

7 Why do some Enduro riders narrow their handlebars? ______________________________

____

8 If you are riding a larger bike on a motocross track, how much distance should there be between your hands on the handlebars?

____

Writing skills

1 This text has a title, a subtitle and a heading. What does this suggest might follow the information about handlebars? ______________________________

____

2 What word in the subtitle sums up the message of the whole text? ____________________

3 Underline what does not apply. The first paragraph could be described as:

a factual **b** informative **c** descriptive

4 In the second paragraph which word first suggests an instructive purpose to this writing?

____

5 Insert the missing letters. 'Pegs' is an example of the use of j _ _ _ _ n in writing.

6 Find another example of jargon in the last paragraph. ____________________

7 Underline all relevant answers. Using this text as an example what does instructive writing lack?

a humour **b** information **c** colour **d** imagery
e description **f** precision **g** technical jargon

8 Underline the correct answer. The writer refers to the riding styles of 'good riders' to:

a offer advice
b dictate a style of riding
c show off his own expertise

9 Underline the correct answer. Remarks such as *in my opinion* and a *good way to start* indicate the writer is instructing by:

a definition **b** suggestion

10 What word throughout the text tells us that the writer is speaking to riders themselves? ____________

11 Underline which of the following is the best description of the tone of this extract.

a coldly factual **b** friendly and informative **c** highly technical

Vocabulary

various	adjust	height	obstruct	sufficient
maximum	leverage	parallel	terrain	sitting

Find all these words in the text you have just read. Make sure you understand their meaning in context, and then learn to spell them using the Look, Cover, Write, Check method. Pay special attention to *leverage* and *parallel*. Spelling rule: If you are adding *~ing* after a syllable with a short vowel you double the last consonant, e.g. *sit—sitting*. If the last syllable has a long vowel you do not double the consonant, e.g. *bite—biting*.

Focus on punctuation

Dashes and hyphens

- Hyphens divide long words to allow them to be finished on another line, e.g. *justifi-cation*
- Hyphens link two closely associated words to form a new word, e.g.
  Peter Pan is a make-believe creation of the writer J.M. Barrie.
- Hyphens can also be used to remove ambiguity, especially in newspaper headlines, e.g.
  Man-eating lion seen near village.
  Without the hyphen, the headline would read as if a man was eating a lion near a village
- Dashes separate an 'aside' from the main statement, e.g.
  Now you add a pinch of salt—where did I put that salt?—and whisk vigorously.
- Dashes separate a list from its explanatory statement, e.g.
  Adidas, Nike, Reebok—they're just expensive labels, that's all!

1 Hyphenate these words appropriately as if you were finishing them on a second line.

a customisation ____________ **b** orchestration ____________

c mountaineering ____________ **d** administratively ____________

2 Rewrite these using a hyphen so that any ambiguity is removed.

a For sale: little used Range Rover. ____________

b a short sighted man ____________

c Carley ordered a hot dog. ____________

3 Insert dashes where appropriate.

a The armies of Napoleon the little man in the three-cornered hat and his hand inside his jacket were defeated by the Russian winter. ____________

____

b If we work through it quietly and carefully Julie! Will you turn that radio down! we'll work it out.

____

c Rude cushions, prat falls, pies in faces these are the stock-in-trade of slapstick comedians.

____

Select a word

Find synonyms from the vocabulary list for the following.

1 impede ____________ **2** enough ____________

3 land ____________ **4** assorted ____________

5 diverse ____________ **6** seated ____________

Grammar

Floating participles

Present participles must always be close to their subjects. If they float around sentences willy-nilly, they cause ambiguity (confuse meaning), e.g.
Walking to school my football was stolen.
floating participle

This is ambiguous. Was the football walking? A correct version would be:
As I was walking to school my football was stolen.
Subject Helping verb and participle following subject

1 Rewrite the following to remove ambiguity following the pattern in the example.

a Crawling into bed the moon rose over the window sill.

____

b Fishing off the jetty the torpedo shape of a grey nurse shark darkened the water.

____

2 Read the following carefully. Rewrite to remove ambiguity where necessary.

a Carving his initials into a park bench a policeman arrested and charged the vandal.

____

b Practising daily Nathan developed into a skilful violinist.

____

c Stopping to sniff the telegraph pole I noticed my dog's collar tag was missing.

____

d Fattened for weeks Ben was really looking forward to a roast turkey dinner.

____

e Running to catch the train I dropped my wallet.

____

Word study

1 Insert an appropriate word from the vocabulary list.

a The stony Gibson Desert is difficult ______________ for walkers.
b I had ______________ money to buy the latest *Dirt Bike* magazine.
c We needed a crowbar for ______________ when we dug out the stump from the Ag. plot.
d The music at our last disco reached the ______________ allowable decibel level.
e Some people complain that skateboarders ______________ the footpath.

2 Add *~ing* to each of the following.

a hit ______________
b shout ______________
c sleep ______________
d clip ______________
e flip ______________
f keep ______________

3 Make nouns of the following by adding suffixes.

a adjust ______________
b obstruct ______________
c sufficient ______________
d various ______________

4 Write antonyms (words that mean the opposite to the given word) for the following. Clues are given for difficult ones.

a maximum ________________ **b** obstruct f _c_ l _ t _ t _

c sufficient ________________ **d** height ________________

e sitting ________________ **f** parallel d _ v _ rg _ nt

5 The prefix *in~* as in *insufficient* is often used to create antonyms. However, when the word begins with 'p' this prefix changes to *im~*, e.g. *polite* ⟶ *impolite*

Make antonyms of these words using the prefix *in~* or *im~*.

a animate ________________ **b** prudent ________________

c efficient ________________ **d** explicit ________________

e patient ________________ **f** capable ________________

Evaluating other people's writing

How to grow potatoes

Find a patch of bare ground, turn it over, check its pH level and fix it up if necessary. Buy your seed potatoes (making sure they're certified) and then plant them in rows. You should be able to get three or four plants out of each potato depending how many eyes they have. Keep them well watered and protected from late frosts. Hill them up as they grow, and when their white flowers die off it will be time to dig up your new potato crop.

1 Is the following information included in the above text? Write 'Yes' or 'No'.

a Where do you buy seed potatoes? ________ **b** What must the potatoes be certified as? ________

c How do you 'fix up' pH levels? ________ **d** When do you plant potatoes? ________

e An explanation of 'hilling'? ________

2 Besides insufficient information, this explanation contains unexplained gardening jargon.

Write two examples of this from the text.________________________ ________________________

Word usage

In English we describe things according to whether they can be counted (number) or heaped (amount) and according to whether they have a definable shape.

- *Much* and *less* describe such things as salt, sand and sunshine.
- *Many* and *few* describe such things as rocks, houses and dogs.

1 Underline the correct alternative.

a We do not have as much/many trees now as in 1788.

b Less/fewer people attended than expected.

c Bushfires were fewer/less last year because of the wet spring.

d That recipe does not use as much/many white pepper as this one.

e This recipe uses just as much/many green peppers as I have in the fridge.

2 Insert an appropriate adjective.

a There was ________________________ salt in the jar than I had hoped.

b Too ________________________ students were interested for the excursion to go ahead.

c Most of the audience stood because there were too ________________________ chairs and too ________________________ people.

d Too ______________________ irrigation causes salinity in the soil.

e Very ______________________ students find grammar exciting.

3 We use specialised measuring words in English.

Match these measuring words to what they measure.

a	fathom	**i**	value of precious stones
b	micron	**ii**	land area
c	carat	**iii**	depth of seawater
d	knot	**iv**	thickness of fleece fibre
e	hectare	**v**	unit of speed at sea

Quick think

Replace the underlined inaccurate words with appropriate and specific nouns or adjectives.

1 Heaps of people were present. ______________________

2 A bunch of elephants quietly grazed. ______________________

3 The biggest lot of Year 8 plays in the quad. ______________________

4 Masses of tiny fish swam under the wharf. ______________________

5 Stacks of boys registered for the Under 15s soccer competition. ______________________

Proofreading

1 Correct misspelt words and add missing punctuation.

Varius hand tools are available for student use. They must be used apropriately are you listening Kylie No chisel can be used for leverege and screwdrivers can't be used to abstruct the movment of any machinery. Now see if you can cut two parrallel 1 cm-deep slits in your wood without choping off any fingers

2 Cross (✗) the sentences that are ambiguous because a present or past participle is floating and tick those that are not ambiguous.

a After descending through the clouds Sydney's red roofs lay beneath us. __

b We visited an exhibition of paintings by Margaret Olley painted in her early years. __

c After descending through the clouds we saw Sydney's red roofs spread out beneath us. __

d We visited an exhibition of Margaret Olley's works that were painted in her early years.__

Idiom

Explain:

1 I wouldn't be in her shoes for anything. ______________________

____

2 I'm sitting on the fence on that issue. ______________________

____

Writing paragraphs and whole texts

1 Read the following explanation. Insert the following words correctly in the blanks.
opportunity, reputable, principle, companions, frequently, mixture, Provide, Handle

Rats make good pets. They are intelligent and with good care can become affectionate and responsive **a**________________. They can be bought from most **b**________________ pet shops for less than ten dollars. A clean, dry and warm cage with plenty of wood shavings on the floor will make a suitable house for your rat. **c**________________ fresh water and a **d**________________ of seed, nuts, fruit and green vegetables daily. Feed small quantities only, as rats quickly become overweight, and provide plenty of **e**________________ for exercise. **f**________________ your rat **g**________________ and gently and it will quickly become attached to you. Rats quickly learn to come when called and to follow simple instructions if taught on the reward-for-response **h**________________.

2 Choose two of the following. Explain how to do them in three clear factual sentences each.

a How to score a game of any sport (only simple scoring, no penalties etc.) **b** How to skateboard

c How to operate a portable CD player **d** How to remove a cork from a bottle

____

____

____

3 You are responsible for the wellbeing of three young bushwalkers you found cold and lost in a deep gorge late in the afternoon. It is too late to lead them out of the gorge before dark, so you must stay the night with them and lead them out in the morning.

Write an explanation of what all four of you must do to survive the night in freezing temperatures well enough to allow you to walk out in the morning. (Think about warmth, shelter from the wind, lifting the spirits of the young walkers etc.). Explain these activities in order of priority.

____

____

____

Chapter test

1 Which sentence is not ambiguous? a __, b __ or c __ ?

a Swimming in the creek an eel bit my toe. **b** As I was swimming in the creek an eel bit my toe.

c An eel bit my toe swimming in the creek.

2 Mark ✗ where you would put the hyphen in this sentence.
Theirs was a long standing friendship.

3 Which sentence is correctly punctuated? a __ or b __ ?

a I'm making an apple pie—pass me the rolling pin, please—from Mum's famous recipe.

b I'm making an apple pie pass me the rolling pin, please from Mum's famous recipe.

4 Circle the correct alternative.
That ring is made of 18 micron/carat gold.

CHAPTER 9

Exposition

STRUCTURE

introduction: indicates subject of text (drink-driving) and writer's own attitude to this subject (negative)

argument: stage 1

conclusion to be drawn from drink-driving blitz results

argument: stage 2 explanation of current drink-driving state of affairs

argument: stage 3 how to improve the situation and deal with offenders

conclusion reinforces the bias ('angle') of the writer towards the subject of drink-driving in this text

The fact that police charged at least 665 NSW motorists with driving under the influence of alcohol during a weekend blitz is appalling and leads to three obvious conclusions.

One, current drink-drive education campaigns are not working.

Two, people still think driving under the influence is an acceptable risk, with the odds in favour of them getting away with it.

Three, current deterrents are plainly not strong enough. By mid-afternoon yesterday police has stopped and tested 76 664 motorists, as part of a three-day blitz which ended at midnight last night.

The 665 positive results represents slightly less than 1 per cent. Projecting this finding, it's possible that at any given time one of every 120 cars or so on NSW roads is in the charge of an alcohol-impaired driver.

A chilling thought.

The Health Department has an informative alcohol education program. Yet too many who undertake it do so as a court directive—that is, after they've been caught. It should be obligatory in our schools or certainly as a prerequisite to obtaining a licence.

Those complacent about ever being caught should realise NSW police conduct more than two million tests a year and are now far more effective and selective—knowing where to operate.

A recent National Drug Strategy survey revealed that 70 per cent of the population admit to having driven while drunk. ... And NSW Traffic Services Commander, Ron Sorenson, says alcohol has replaced speed as the biggest killer on our roads.

Sobering statistics.

So how do we stop it? It's plain drink-drivers are not responding to education programs, which tell them at which stage their blood alcohol content exceeds the limit.

Increasing numbers of convictions do not impress them. It'll never happen to them, they say.

So it's down to penalties. And the current ones (fine and suspension) are no longer enough.

The Northern Territory's harsh mandatory sentencing legislation—which inflicts prison terms on first offenders in a blanket crackdown on crime—may be controversial, but it certainly works.

Drink-drivers are potential killers. More should be jailed.

They are criminals and should be treated as such.

LANGUAGE FEATURES

- *explanatory*
- *biased towards one view of the subject*
- *persuasive*

fact (blitz) and opinion ('appalling' test-positive results) mixed and presented as fact

numbering of conclusions gives impression of reasoned argument

numbers and projection of numbers gives impression of factual accuracy

single phrase directs reader's response to preceding argument and allows writer to begin a new stage of argument

use of statistics and quoted authorities adds note of truth and reliability to argument

question involving personal pronoun 'we' involves reader in solving the problem

simple colloquial sentences involve reader and invite agreement with writer's solution to problem of drink-drivers

short direct statements suggest decision and unarguable fact

Comprehension

1 Underline the correct answer. This editorial is an exposition of the view that:

a there should be a renewed drink-driving education campaign

b police are to be criticised for failing to crack down on drink-driving

c drink-drivers should be punished more severely

d breath-testing locations should be chosen more carefully

2 How many conclusions has the writer reached about the state of drink-driving in NSW?

____

3 To what do the words *665 positive results* refer?

a the number of cars on NSW roads

b the number of drivers tested during the blitz

c the number of tested drivers who returned a positive reading

4 Why has the Health Department's alcohol education program largely failed?

____

5 Of the Australian driving population, 70% have driven while drunk. Is this true or false? ______________

6 Underline the correct alternative. Drink-driving convictions have increased/decreased since 1994.

7 Underline the correct answer. The solution to NSW drink-driving is:

a adopt the Northern Territory's mandatory sentencing legislation

b jail all offenders **c** increase fines and suspension periods

d treat offenders as potential killers and criminals

Writing skills

1 What three words in the first paragraph tell us that this piece of writing is going to be an exposition (explanation) of a particular point of view?

____

2 What word in the first paragraph suggests that this point of view is an outraged one? ______________

3 Underline the answer that does not apply. The use of numbers to count off the conclusions gives an impression of:

a logic **b** careful thought **c** organisation of argument **d** lazy writing

4 What evidence is offered to support the argument that too many people are still drinking and driving?

____

5 The figure *slightly less than 1 per cent* would usually be considered low. How does the writer explain that figure to ensure readers understand that too many drivers are still driving under the influence of alcohol?

____

6 Underline the correct answer. The effect of the phrase *A chilling thought* is to:

a ensure readers respond with concern to the picture described

b provide a breathing space in the argument

7 Find another phrase which performs the same function at a similar point in the text.

____

8 Underline the correct answer. The first stage of the exposition is:

a a drink-driving blitz

b conclusions about drink-driving in NSW based on blitz results

c the assertion that people drink and drive because they think they can get away with it

9 Underline the correct answer. The middle stage of the argument mainly concerns:

a facts about drink-driving prevention **b** statistics about drink-driving

c reasons for drink-driving preventive measures not working

10 Which line begins the third stage of the exposition (how we should deal with drink-drivers)?

____

11 Underline the correct answer. The final sentence:

a sums up the **premise** (main idea) behind the exposition

b is rather exaggerated in the light of what precedes it

c is unnecessarily harsh

12 Underline the two most appropriate answers. Overall the tone of this piece of writing could be described as:

a annoyed **b** outraged **c** sarcastic **d** dogmatic

Vocabulary

appalling	**deterrent**	**favour**	**alcohol**	**statistics**
mandatory	**impaired**	**complacent**	**prerequisite**	**controversial**

Circle the doubled consonants in the first two words as an aid to spelling recall. *Alcohol* is often misspelt, as is *statistics,* because students add extra letters. Practise these words very carefully. When you are sure of them ask someone to hear you spell them. Both words occur frequently in your science and health subjects at school.

Focus on punctuation

Apostrophe of contraction

- An **apostrophe** takes the place of missing letters in an abbreviated word, e.g.
  they are > they're *it is > it's*
- *It is* is abbreviated to *it's*. You must take care not to confuse this with *its*, a possessive form of the personal pronoun *it*, e.g.
  That's not a cat; it's a possum. The possum has a baby on its back.
- This kind of abbreviation is called a **contraction**.

1 Insert apostrophes of abbreviation in the following.

a theyre going ________________ **b** were here ________________

c hes outside ________________ **d** Im running ________________

e youre a loser ________________ **f** shes already left ________________

2 Insert apostrophes of abbreviation where necessary.

a Were all going to Coffs Harbour for Christmas.

b Those arent the usual brand of joggers I wear.

c I wouldve brought it if you had rung me to ask.

d The orphan wombat hadnt been fed for some time.

3 Write the correct abbreviations of the following.

a have not ____________________ b should have ____________________

c could have ____________________ d might not ____________________

e need not ____________________ f you are ____________________

4 Underline the correct alternative.

a The snake shed it's/its skin in spring. b A lioness shares it's/its prey with the cubs.

c The microphone is not here; it's/its over there. d Its/it's not what you asked; it's/its how you asked that offended me.

5 Write *its* or *it's* as appropriate in the spaces.

a I don't know whether _____ going to rain today.

b If _____ wet, the school will follow the alternative program for the day.

c The flag has snapped _____ halyard in the wind.

d Many a ship has lost _____ cargo after being caught in a typhoon.

e We don't know whether _____ a lost dog or whether _____ thoughtless owner has just let it out for a run.

Select a word

Find an antonym (opposite) for each of the following from the list words in the vocabulary list.

1 inducement ____________________ **2** optional ____________________

3 discontented ____________________ **4** popular ____________________

5 generalisations ____________________ **6** appealing ____________________

Grammar

Verb forms that act like adjectives

Another way of joining two simple sentences into one is by the use of a verb form that acts like an adjective, e.g.

The child was crying. The child's mother cuddled it.
The mother cuddled her crying child.

The fish was netted. The fish was measured and returned to the water.
The netted fish was measured and returned to the water.

1 Underline the verb forms that act like adjectives in the following.

a An ambulance officer attended the weeping accident victim. b Amanda is an aspiring actress.

c Students appreciate a smiling Principal. d The woman was distressed. She wrung her hands and wept.

e Henry's horse was injured. The vet attended the horse.

2 Join the sentences in each example by using a verb form as an adjective (make any other necessary changes).

a The lead singer was shrieking. The clamour of her 40-decibel accompaniment drowned her out.

____

b A sea eagle seized a mutton-bird chick. The mutton-bird chick was screeching in its nest.

____

c A youth was skateboarding in Johnson Street. The youth saved a child from being run over by a truck.

____

d The children were laughing. They played beach cricket on the sand.

____

e Penguins lay dying on the beach. The penguins were covered in oil from a spill at sea.

____

f The cards were shuffled. The dealer passed them out to the players.

____

g Shellfish were gathered. The shellfish were then packed in ice.

____

Word study

1 Match a word from the vocabulary list to each meaning.

a damaged, functioning poorly __________ b causing disagreement __________

c discouragement __________ d satisfied, unworried __________

2 Insert an appropriate word from the vocabulary list in the following.

a His __________ injuries will keep him in hospital for several months.

b __________ show that young female drivers are nearly as dangerous as young male drivers on the road.

c The weather will be in our __________ if we drive to Alice Springs in winter.

d Detentions are a common __________ for misbehaviour at school.

3 Are the following underlined words used correctly in these sentences? Write 'Yes' or 'No'.

a Bicycle helmets are mandatory in NSW. __________

b His vision was impaired by the wearing of prescription glasses to improve his sight. __________

c Liking sushi is a prerequisite for studying Advanced Japanese. __________

d Mrs Hoy was ecstatically complacent when she heard she had won the lottery. __________

4 Find synonyms for these words in the list.

a damaged __________ b grace __________

c compulsory __________ d dreadful __________

Evaluating other people's writing

Submission in support of a geology excursion

In our science course we are studying alpine geology in Australia. We think we should go there. We would learn much better there.

We could go swimming in Lake Jindabyne and if we go in November the chairlifts might still be operating so we could see all out across the range. There's hostels where students can stay and the guides there can tell us all about aplite and those other rocks like quartz that you can see on the hills.

Mr Jones thinks geology is a hands-on subject so an excursion would be a good way of doing it. We could go trout fishing too. Sam Smith's father says he could lend us all the fly-fishing gear we would need so it wouldn't cost the school anything.

Our science class is sure that we will have a great time and we promise that we will behave well.

The submission above seeks to persuade a school Principal that a geology excursion to the Snowy Mountains would be educationally beneficial. However, it will not persuade the Principal because it is a very poor piece of expository writing.

1 Underline all the errors of expository writing below that occur in this passage.

a lack of logical argument
b haphazard organisation
c insufficient evidence
d lack of interest in the intended subject
e lack of precision in factual detail
f irrelevant statements
g inappropriate conclusion
h absence of premise behind argument

2 This submission also contains obvious examples of poor expression. Find:

a an incorrect verb ______________________

b an illogical combination of ideas in one sentence (number the paragraph and the sentence)

____

c an irrelevant statement ____

d unconnected adverbs in the second and third sentences of the first paragraph.

____

e unnecessary adverbs in the first sentence of the second paragraph ______________________

Word usage

Redundancy occurs when two words are saying the same thing. One word is therefore redundant or unnecessary, e.g.
We followed behind them. (To follow means to travel behind, so *behind* is redundant in this sentence.)

1 Underline the redundant word or phrase.

a Once more he climbed up the tree again.
b Mrs O'Hara returned back to her homeland.
c As a rule Jane usually opens all the windows.
d Bass and Flinders circumnavigated around Australia.
e He vowed to defend and safeguard her all his days.

2 *Can* means able to, e.g. *I can play mah-jong.*
May means allowed to, e.g. *You may go to Peter's to play mah-jong.*
Insert *can* or *may* appropriately.

a ______________________ I go to the movies on Saturday?

b She's a brain. She ______________________ even understand algebra.

c Yes, you ______________________ join the band but you must come to practice at lunchtime.

d ______________________ you hold the ladder steady or is it too heavy?

3 Using your dictionary for reference, underline the correct alternative of these often confused terms.

a A biennial event happens:
i twice yearly **ii** every two years

b A bimonthly magazine is published:
i twice monthly **ii** every two years

c A perennial plant flowers:
i every year **ii** only in one year

d an annual plant flowers:
i every year **ii** only in one year

4 The words *explain*, *clarify* and *elucidate* are all associated with making something clearly understood. Insert one of these words in an appropriate space.

a The teacher handed out maps to ____________ just what region he was talking about.

b Can you ______________ how you came by this ten dollar note?

c I need some more information to _______________ this problem.

Quick think

1 These Greek words are the basis of many English words. Using them, write words to match the meanings below: *chronos* (time), *cosmos* (world), *ge* (earth), *anthropos* (man):

a timed sequence of events ______________________

b a Russian astronaut ______________________

c the study of the earth's structure ______________________

d the study of human society ______________________

e a very precise clock ______________________

f at home in any city of world ______________________

2 Group these words under the headings below. Some may belong under two headings.

bench, flock, milestone, sericulture, tonne, precedent, sentence, calving, scales, instant, knot, aquaculture, wig, acquittal, apiarist, pedometer, micron, verdict, justice, nanosecond, swine, furlong, remand, millennium, litre, sundial, stables

Time	**Law**	**Measurement**	**Husbandry**

Proofreading

Correct the spelling and punctuation.

The fixing of P plates to the cars of newly licenced drivers is mandatary for the first year of driving. During that period a P-plated driver may consume no alchahol at all prior to or while driving. Neither can such a driver exced 80 kilometres an hour.

Thats unfair many young drivers complain citing the fact that many older drivers are anything but good drivers. However stastistics quite clearly prove that youth and exsessive speed are a common and dangrous combination on our roads, almost as lethel as the combination of drinking and driving.

Idiom

Explain:

1 That canister is sealed tight as a drum. ______________________

____

2 I wouldn't give tuppence for what he thinks. ______________________

____

Writing paragraphs and whole texts

1 Write an introduction to an exposition defending the claim of students to discounted tickets at celebrity concerts. In your introduction, make your view of the present pricing system clear and what you want in its place. Be very clear in your explanation and in your statement of what you want.

2 Write a conclusion to an exposition which asserts that children no longer have sufficient leisure time, suggesting that creative leisure classes be timetabled in school curriculums.

3 Write a five-point plan for an exposition on one of the following topics.

a that teenagers have more sense than they are given credit for
b that computer games teach eye–hand coordination, manual dexterity and rapid reasoning
c that skateboarding takes real skill

Chapter test

1 Insert the missing hyphen in this sentence: Panning for gold is a hands on occupation.

2 Which sentence is correct? a __ or b __?

a That cat has lost it's bell collar. **b** That cat has lost its bell collar.

3 Join these sentences using a verb form as an adjective.
A hawk was watching. The hawk dived on a field mouse in the grass.

4 Insert the missing apostrophe in this sentence.
We know where youre going.

CHAPTER 10

Interview

An interview with Tony Joe White

The pictures on your CD cover define what I imagine the swamplands to be like. Was it like that where you grew up?

Yeh, it's kinda like that around my parts now too. I was kinda in the north end, the Delta part, but we had to go through the rivers and swamps. That picture on the back is down close to a little town called Napoleonville outside of New Orleans about 40 miles.

You like to write about characters. Are they always real people?

Mostly all the characters through the years have been real, every one of them, from Polk Salad Annie to Gumbo John (a character in a song off the new album who used to play guitar until his pet alligator Clyde took a liking to his fingers). In fact, that shack where I'm sittin' on the porch on the back of the album cover, that's Gumbo John's shack. He owns the house and right across the road is his cafe right on the water.

Another character you sing about on One Hot July *is the Conjure Woman, but I notice the copyright on that is from 1970.*

I did it back in the 'Polk' days but never really cut it the way I wanted to cut it. There was something about going back to Louisiana and gettin' back in the swamps. That studio is in the middle of 50 acres of swampland and it's an old log house that this guy has had since early 60s. I said man, this is where I need to re-do 'The Conjure Woman'. There's still a lot of that [Voodoo] still going on down there.

What is your song-writing process?

Most of the time it's like a guitar lick will start it for me. I'll be playing the guitar, then once I get an idea I'll build me a little camp fire outside, get a couple of cold beers and sit out there and work a while. But I usually wait till a guitar lick comes or a title or a line. I don't never just sit down and say I'm going to write a song, something has to happen first. I've got a little 16 track here in my studio and when I get ready to put it down, me and my drummer, 'Boom Boom', will come in and lay something down. The songs and the lines usually stick in my head if they're good enough.

Have you been using the same guitar all these years?

It's an old Strat. I've had it for a long time. I don't know how long and I've got an old '58. The one I use mostly is a '61. I used a Spanish guitar a couple of times on this album. It's a '69 Spanish that I write a lot of tunes on. That's the one I carry out to the camp fire. The amplifier is a Blues Deville.

Do you use many effects?

Only the old whomper. The old boomerang wha and a thing called a Colourtone that I bought in London England back in '69. I use those two and that's about it.

Is it difficult for you to say that a record is finally finished and not want to do anything else to it?

You know I have a really great cut-off valve, man, when I'm through with one in the studio. Even in the early days, when it's making everyone feel good and we're all smiling and standin' around listening to it, the musicians and I, I know it's through right then. I don't keep trying to tangle with it.

Greg Phillips, *Australian Musician*

STRUCTURE

prepared questions seeking answers that will encourage interviewee to reveal himself

introduction establishes background

body of interview

A = the songs

B = the song-writing and recording process

conclusion: brings songs and song writing together to end interview

LANGUAGE FEATURES

questions brief and precise; designed to have interviewee reveal himself

word 'swamplands' directs interviewee's answer (not his life elsewhere, only that childhood Louisiana area)

accurate recording of colloquial language

statement of fact establishes what interviewer wants writer to talk about

statement acting as a question; open so White can respond as he chooses

humour to enliven interview

precise question for a specific answer

dialect and technical phrases—make interview 'live' for reader

technical facts for the country-music fan

question implies understanding of White's psyche; flatters him

colloquialisms

Comprehension

1 Underline the correct answer. White is:

a an Australian **b** a Canadian **c** an American **d** an Englishman

2 What is White's instrument? ______________________

3 Underline the correct answer. White's current CD is called:

a 'The Conjure Woman' **b** *One Hot July*

4 Insert the missing words. The songs on that CD are all based on life in ______________________

5 What was it about his home territory that White needed to get 'The Conjure Woman' right?

____

6 The amplifier White uses is *an old Strat* he has had for a long time. True/False ____

7 White's production effects are very sophisticated. Is this true or false? ______________________

8 Underline the correct answer. The moment of record completion:

a is clear **b** takes a lot of rethinking to arrive at **c** is arbitrary **d** is a matter of instinct

9 What does White mean when he says: *I don't keep trying to tangle with it*? ______________________

____

Writing skills

1 Underline the wrong answer. Phillips' first question is designed to:

a establish the background to the CD **b** put White at his ease

c provoke an interesting answer **d** identify the scene on the CD cover

2 Which question establishes that Phillips is a well-informed interviewer and deserving of the interviewee's respect? ______________________

3 Underline two correct answers. Phillips quotes White **verbatim** (exactly). This is:

a lazy interviewing practice **b** observant interviewing practice

c an indication of poor editing **d** an assistance to the reader in really understanding White

4 Underline the correct answer. Phillips' questions are very short and White's answers are extended. Is this:

a evidence of good interviewing technique? **b** evidence of poor interviewer preparation?

5 Questions 1, 2 and 3 contain statements followed by questions. This:

a allows the interviewer to shape the kind of answer given

b allows the interviewer to sound knowledgeable **c** is unimaginative questioning style

6 Phillips sets out to discover three things in this interview. Underline which three of the following.

a how White writes songs **b** what inspires his song writing

c the recording process **d** how White's songs are produced

e the character of Swamplands territory

7 Questions establish background, fact and opinion. Which question establishes the background for this interview? ______________________

8 Underline the most important answer. Phillips includes White's reference to Gumbo John's alligator and his finger food preference, even though it has no bearing on the CD being discussed, to:

a add interest to the interview **b** fill space

c catch the character of the man and his music **d** explain the CD cover

9 Underline the correct answer. The tone of this interview is:

a aggressive **b** friendly **c** critical

10 Underline any incorrect answer. The language of this interview is:

a all jargon **b** direct **c** colloquial **d** part of its appeal

11 Underline two correct answers. The purpose of this interview is to:

a persuade **b** inform **c** entertain **d** argue

Vocabulary

guitar	**imagine**	**character**	**alligator**	**studio**
presentation	**technique**	**style**	**research**	**verbatim**

Words in the top row of the vocabulary list occur in the text. They are all simple words but their spelling is tricky. Words in the bottom row of the vocabulary list are all concerned with aspects of interviewing. Make sure you know to what they refer. Then learn to spell them, using the Look, Cover, Write, Check method.

Focus on punctuation

Brackets and dashes

- Brackets and dashes both enclose asides and short explanations of something already said, e.g.
  The band (so Mr Smith reminded me) is practising this afternoon.
  We will be playing at Queen's Park—the one by the river—at 2 o'clock.
- Dashes also separate a sentence into two parts, with one part being a comment on the other, e.g.
  That wretched rooster—I'll wring its noisy neck!
  Don't just tell me—show me.
- In note making, dashes separate each idea from the next, e.g.
  Do dishes—Feed dog—Buy bread—Collect mail.

Insert brackets and dashes as necessary.

1 The book was in the library and that surprised me since it is so popular so I could finish reading it.

2 She always cooks with oil not just any old oil, mind you, but cholesterol-free canola oil because she says it enhances the flavour of the dish.

3 Tweet! Tweet! Tweet! That budgie's driving me insane put it outside.

4 The Southern Lights scientists call them Aurora Australis are a spectacular atmospheric light display over the Antarctic.

5 Ring Ali Write to Sarah Return Kevin's book Finish assignment.

6 That stopwatch belonging to the coach where did I put it?

Select a word

Choose from *bipedal, biennial, exhume, examine, excavate, Neolithic, neonate* to match the following.

1 to dig out ______________________

2 to remove from a grave ______________________

3 having two feet ______________________

4 from the New Stone Age ______________________

5 happening every two years ______________________

6 newborn infant ______________________

Grammar

Prepositions

- **Prepositions** are small words that locate things or actions, in time and place and in relation to each other, e.g.
  That cat has raced onto the table, under the chair, behind the couch, beyond my reach, through the window and into the yard.
- Prepositions follow a verb and precede a noun or pronoun, as in *raced onto the table.*
  Verb Preposition Noun
- Some verbs are followed by specific prepositions. The most common of these are: *differ from, compare with, liaise with, inquire of, insist on, to die of (something)*
- Some adjectives are also followed by specific prepositions. The most common of these are: *different from* (**never** different than), *identical to, similar to*

1 Underline all the prepositions.

a The band's instruments were stacked against the wall.

b Inside a tin chest were kept all the old records sealed in oiled paper.

c Tony Joe White went back to Louisiana to rewrite 'The Conjure Woman'.

d Australian country singers are recognised on the American country circuit.

e Tubas and trombones play beside each other in an orchestra.

2 Insert an appropriate preposition.

a Is that a gift ______________________ your girlfriend?

b The speed boat raced ______________________ the horizon and disappeared _______ it.

c Year 8 drifted ______________________ the quadrangle aimlessly.

d 'A lap means ______________________ the oval, not ______________________ it!' roared the coach.

e He looked ______________________ the door ______________________ the yellowed paddocks.

3 Complete these sentences with the correct proposition.

a How does your answer differ _____ mine?

b Our team manager will liaise _____ the manager of the visiting team about refreshments.

c I am going to inquire _____ the Council the details of when our road will be repaired.

d Until the development of antibiotics many people died _____ infection.

e Paul's new fishing rod is identical _____ his father's.

4 The underlined prepositions are incorrect. One preposition is missing altogether. Write the correct or missing preposition in the space.

a That green frog is different than this one, which has yellow stripes. ________

b Oranges, compared to lemons, are the same shape but have a different colour. ________

c I will write __ you when I get there. ________

d Our principal was angry at the students who had misbehaved on the bus. ________

e Those twins, Sam and Ian, are identical with each other. ________

Word study

1 Match words from the bottom row of the vocabulary list to the following.

a quoted exactly as said ______________________

b manner or way of doing something ______________________

c a particular skill or process ______________________

d information gathering ______________________

e appearance of the final product ______________________

2 Insert words appropriately from the bottom row of the vocabulary list.

a A police record of interview is always transcribed ______________________.

b An aggressive interviewing ______________________ will antagonise an interviewee.

c Experienced interviewers always ______________________ known information about the subject before the interview.

d Statement followed by question is a useful interviewing ______________________.

e The transcript ______________________ of an interview depends on such factors as availability of photographs, font style and print size.

3 The following words have Greek and Latin prefixes: *neo~* (new), *ex~* (out of), *bi~* (two), *quad~* (four). Complete words meaning:

a to cut in two bi _ _ _ _

b a newborn baby neo _ _ _ _

c to breathe out ex _ _ _ _

d a four-sided geometric figure quad _ _ _ _ _ _ _ _ _

e to drive out from a homeland ex _ _ _

f a two-wheeled pedalled vehicle bi _ _ _ _ _

g a four-sided courtyard quad _ _ _ _ _ _

4 Insert words appropriately from the top row of the vocabulary list.

a An ________________, superficially, is very like a crocodile.

b Very few can ________________ just how complex our Australian ecosystems are.

c A ________________ is where an artist in any discipline creates her work.

d The ________________ belongs to the stringed family of musical instruments.

e Experience is what shapes the ________________ of a person.

Evaluating other people's writing

An interview with Sam Holt, writer of Westerns

Sam, are you an American?

No, I was born in New Zealand

What is your best story?

'Denver Red'.

How many stories have you written?

About thirty.

Some people are compulsive writers. They really like writing and wouldn't be doing anything else. How do you feel about writing?

I'm one of those writers. I really enjoy writing and I'm so lucky that I get paid for doing something that I like doing, something I'd still be doing even if it didn't pay financially.

Do you get paid heaps?

No.

1 Which question evoked the most revealing answer in this interview? ______________________

2 Underline the correct answer. This kind of question:

a asks for a fact **b** is open-ended **c** require a yes/no answer

3 Underline the correct answer. Which of the following would have been a more productive second question?

a So how does a Kiwi come to write Westerns? **b** Were you brought up in America?

c Have you researched the American West?

4 Underline appropriate answers. The final question is:

a ill-mannered and intrusive **b** poorly expressed

c not very relevant **d** good challenging interviewing style

Word usage

Look back to 'Word usage' in Chapter 8 if necessary before answering these questions.

1 Underline the correct alternative.

a How many/much apples are left?

b I was surprised by the amount/number of people present.

c There were less/fewer rings on display than expected.

d The bulk/majority of Australian country music stars have played at the Tamworth Country Music Festival.

2 Insert an appropriate number or bulk word.

a That recipe calls for ______________________ flour than others I have used.

b The ______________________ of sky divers is aged below 40.

c Teenagers eat an alarming ______________________ of salty food.

d How ______________________ days notice of resignation are required in your job?

3 Write antonyms (opposites) for these number and quantity words:

a more ______________________ **b** many ______________________

c majority ______________________ **d** most ______________________

e maximum ______________________ **f** surplus ______________________

4 Choose an appropriate group or bulk word and write it in the space.

couplet, nest, quatrain, gallons, clutch, litres, school, dozen, flotilla, score

a Penny raised a ___________ of chickens in a box under a light

b An egg carton usually contains a ___________ eggs.

c Two lines of rhyming verse are called a ___________.

d A ___________ of sailing ships cruised into the harbour.

e Petrol is measured in ___________.

5 Arrange these time counting words in order of least to greatest.

hour nanosecond minute second microsecond

____

Quick think

1 Complete the following, which relate to the music scene.

a an engagement to perform — g _ g

b on a trip to perform musically — on t _ _ _

c one who looks after a band's finances and engagement bookings — m _ _ _ _ _ r

d equipment to increase sound level of music — a _ _ _ _ _ _ _ _

e where CDs are recorded — s _ _ _ _ _

f the idea a songwriter must have to write a song — i _ _ p _ _ ation

2 Some musical directions have passed into everyday language. Can you match these common musical expressions to the examples on the left?

tempo, presto, a cappella, staccato, crescendo

a rapid, sharp clear sounds in sequence as in machine-gun fire ______________

b often uttered by magicians when something appears unexpectedly ______________

c growing steadily louder ______________

d beat or rhythm ______________

e singing in a group unaccompanied by instruments ______________

Proofreading

Correct misspellings and incorrect usage, and insert any missing punctuation.

Studeo recording can be exhausting Musicians as well the studio staff need to understand the tecknicqes of recording to ensure a good recording. Not much stars have there own studeo as White has and the bulk of them have to rely on the skills of whatever studio they can persuade to like their stile and sound. This probly sounds depressing it's just show business.

Idiom

Explain:

1 After Tom's first drum performance the lead singer said he was worth his weight in gold to the band.

____

2 The boys were at a loss to explain how their dog esaped from a gated and locked yard. ______________

____

Writing paragraphs and whole texts

1 Your student newspaper has sent you to interview the sports Head Teacher about the new and exciting sports that are rumoured to have been added to a previously dreary sports program. Write the opening question for that interview.

____

2 Imagine a car accident in your neighbourhood. Write five questions a newspaper reporter might ask an eyewitness.

____

____

____

____

____

3 Imagine one of the following scenarios.

a A teenager has saved her friend from drowning in a stormwater channel.

b A youth has been awarded a bravery medal for saving a child from a burning house.

Write a record of an interview with one of these brave people. Include both questions and answers. To distinguish the speakers, use print for one and handwriting for the other.

____

____

____

____

____

____

____

____

____

____

____

Chapter test

1 Which sentence is correct? a __ or b __?

a This album is different than his first hit album, *Snow in Summer.*

b This album is different from his first hit album, *Snow in Summer.*

2 Circle the misspelt word in this sentence.

His fingering tecnique does not suit a guitar.

3 Which sentence is correctly punctuated? a __ or b __?

a The Berlin Symphony Orchestra the one that's visiting Sydney now is playing at the Opera House tonight.

b The Berlin Symphony Orchestra (the one that's visiting Sydney now) is playing at the Opera House tonight.

4 Circle the correct alternative.

Too much/many cooks will spoil the broth.

CHAPTER 11

Music review

STRUCTURE

purpose: to discuss strengths and weaknesses and then recommend or condemn

album

artist and recording company

introduction (very brief)

body of review:

***A** the artist*

***B** the new album*

conclusion: summary and recommendation

reviewer byline

Nothing to hide

***Felicity*—EMI**

Having high expectations placed on your first album means that it generally comes under closer scrutiny than most.

For Aussie country singer/songwriter Felicity, the title of her new album, *Nothing To Hide*, may also typify her approach to music.

And, just like the artist, this album is fresh, enthusiastic and very appealing.

Felicity has certainly come of age with this album and for those expecting an album full of songs in the vein of her hit cover 'Sugar Town', you'll be pleasantly surprised.

There are 13 tracks on the album plus a bonus 'dance version' of 'Sugar Town'.

The first couple of tracks, 'Amazing' and 'Counting Back the Days', have a distinct Olivia Newton-John sound to them.

Felicity says that this was completely unintentional but for the listener it's uncanny. She continues the rural theme with her hit 'Country Girl' and then goes on to show that she is an artist of substance with some very strong ballads, especially the duet with Rick Price, 'If You Were My Baby'.

She ventures off the path with a Mariachi number called 'That's What I Call Love' which has hit potential as well and includes a tribute to one of her idols, John Williamson, and to warmer climates with JW's song 'Tropical Fever'.

Nothing To Hide is one of those albums which could have as much appeal to contemporary charts as it will to country charts and should win Felicity plenty of fans, no matter what their musical tastes.

Bob Anthony in *Country Update* magazine

LANGUAGE FEATURES

compact statement

positive adjectives

inducement

concise phrase implying much

musical jargon

double example of appeal underlines recommendation

Comprehension

1 Felicity is well known on the country music scene. Is this true or false? ____________________

2 If *Nothing To Hide* is Felicity's first album, why does Anthony describe her as having *come of age* with its production? ____________________

____

3 Felicity is a solo artist on this album. Is this true or false? ____________________

4 What is the connection with Olivia Newton-John? ____________________

5 Underline which of these best describes the album.

a pure country **b** middle-of-the-road **c** appealing to a wide range of musical tastes

6 How many tracks are there on this new album? ______________________

7 Give at least two reasons why we know Felicity is a country and western singer.

a ____

b ____

8 If a song is called a ballad we know it tells a _ _ _ _ _.

9 Underline the correct answer. Felicity's songs are:

a written as simple lyrics **b** written as ballads **c** written in several styles

Writing skills

1 Which part of the text carries all the necessary detail for a would-be buyer of this album?

____

2 Paragraph 1 conveys the most important fact in this review. What is it? ______________________

____

3 Insert the missing word.

We realise this is going to be a positive review as early as the ______________ paragraph.

4 Underline the correct answer. The word *appealing* here means:

a pleasantly attractive **b** dramatically attractive **c** challengingly attractive

5 Underline the *incorrect* answer. The reference to 'Sugar Town' is intended to:

a recall a well-received song **b** establish a recognition factor

c show a development of singing range **d** indicate an improvement on previous performance

6 Write two examples of musical recording jargon that occur in this review.

______________ ______________

7 Suggest why Anthony makes reference to Olivia Newton-John in this review.

____

8 Underline the correct answer. The phrase *an artist of substance* is:

a slight praise **b** serious approval

9 Underline the correct answer. *She ventures off the path with …* is an example of:

a simile **b** metaphor **c** comparison **d** alliteration

10 What words in the final paragraph tell us that Felicity's album will appeal to fans of pop music as well as country music?

____

11 Underline the correct answer. The tone of this review is:

a generally favourable **b** very positive **c** uncritical **d** mildly critical

Vocabulary

expectation	typify	scrutiny	venture	version
potential	duet	contemporary	tribute	unintentional

Locate these words in the text and work out their meaning in context. Then break them into syllables for ease of memorisation. Pay special attention to *typify* and *contemporary*, which are often misspelt.

Focus on punctuation

Direct speech

- **Direct speech** is a person's spoken words. It is enclosed in inverted commas. If more than one person is speaking, you begin a new paragraph each time the speaker changes, e.g.
  'Do you want to play soccer tonight, Frank?' asked Steven.
  'No, thanks. I'm going running with my brother tonight.'
- If words like *he said, she replies, they yelled* etc. precede direct speech, a comma is placed after them, e.g.
  When he dropped the hammer from the roof Mr Aboud shouted, 'Watch out!'

1 Insert all necessary punctuation, using [to indicate a new paragraph.

a Please may I have a go No Why not Because I said so That's why

b That's the best joke I've heard in a long time laughed Bob. Why don't you tell Mr George in Geography It might even get us out of that test

c Move along now There's nothing to see here said the policeman as he ushered the crowd away from the door

2 Correct or complete the punctuation of the following.

a 'That's not my bag? she shrieked.

b Why is that window opened? his mother asked.

c 'Can't imagine where I left it muttered the voice in the dark!

3 Rewrite the following text on the lines below, punctuating all direct speech correctly. (Don't forget paragraphs.)

Do you want to go to the ABBA concert down at the hall tonight? ABBA doesn't exist any more, Amy told me bluntly. Yes, I know that, but this group sings all the ABBA songs and dresses like them too. Come on, it'll be a good night, I promise you. Oh, all right, I suppose anything's better than watching reruns on TV said Amy with a smile.

____

____

____

____

____

Select a word

Find a synonym for the following words from the vocabulary list.

1 accidental ______________

2 possibility ______________

3 recognition ______________

4 anticipation ______________

5 dare or attempt ______________

6 grant or praise ______________

Grammar

Prepositions for special situations

As we learned in Chapter 10, some words take only one correct preposition after them. These include *bored with*, *tolerant of*, *embarrassed by*.

1 Underline the correct preposition.

- **a** P.E. teachers are more tolerant with/of loud music than other teachers.
- **b** She was embarrassed at/by her friend's continued talking in the library.
- **c** Smithy is renowned for his knowledge of/on sporting trivia.
- **d** I was bored of/with watching cricket.
- **e** Trent borrowed cricket pads from/off Gavin.

2 American speech patterns have led to some confusion about the use or non-use of prepositions. The following sentences are incorrect in Australian English. Rewrite them correctly by adding, changing or eliminating prepositions.

- **a** We met with Leo and Paul at Circular Quay.

  ____

- **b** Lauren promised to write me as soon as she reached Bourke.

  ____

- **c** The demonstration was held to protest the ban on the wearing of earrings.

  ____

3 From these prepositions choose appropriate ones to fill each blank.
through, under, of, to, beyond, beneath, over, on, within

- **a** I am susceptible ____________ respiratory infections.
- **b** He is dependent ____________ his brother's help.
- **c** She lives ____________ her means.
- **d** Mr Jones was unaware ____________ Elaine's presence.
- **e** Players were selected ____________ their merits.

Word study

1 Find words from the vocabulary list that mean the same as these words.

- **a** something greater than hope ____________
- **b** a piece played by two people together ____________
- **c** a very close inspection ____________
- **d** a particular rendition of a song or a story ____________

2 Insert adjectives from the vocabulary list.

- **a** The music of the last few years could be called ____________ music.
- **b** This racehorse is a ____________ champion.
- **c** My breaking that ornament was completely ____________.

3 Read the following examples.

- *The bronzed lifesaver is said to typify the Australian male.*
- *The word 'mate' is considered to typify the Australian attitude of regarding all people as equal.*

Now underline what the word *typify* means:

a to represent **b** to exaggerate **c** to mock **d** to denigrate

4 If you were to *venture* to do something this would imply that one of the following would be involved. Underline which one.

a anger **b** courage **c** confidence **d** uncertainty

5 Some words can be both nouns and verbs, e.g. *venture* as a verb can mean to risk or attempt and as a noun it means an enterprise with some degree of risk attached.
These words can be nouns or verbs. Insert them in the spaces in the following sentences.
attempt, pluck, plans, auction

a He plans to ____________ off his farm to the highest bidder.

b The ____________ of the house next door was attended by lots of potential buyers.

c Her first ____________ at playing jazz was a disaster.

d Holly ________a solo album to follow the success of her latest song on community radio.

e Guitarists do not always __________ their strings with their fingers; they often use a plectrum to do so.

f The police commended the little boy for his __________ in facing down the dog that threatened his sister.

Evaluating other people's writing

1 Read this passage carefully and insert the following in the blanks.

broke, Outstanding, impact, potential, released, inception

a____________________ Australian country music star Lee Kernaghan has been announced as the Country Music Radio's 'Hitmaker of the Decade' following his dominance of CMR's Country Tracks Charts since their **b**____________________ 10 years ago.

Admittedly Lee has mainly enjoyed his success from 1992 onwards when his *Boys from the Bush* was **c**____________________. Since then he has charted 20 times and every track, including his duets, has reached the top 10 with 14 going on to make the top spot.

Manager of CMR, Nick Erby, said that Lee's **d**____________________ on the charts was all the more significant because all the other leading chartmakers have all had hits since 1989. That meant Lee had a three-year 'catch-up' period.

The CMR honour comes on top of Lee's being awarded the 1999 APRA Most Performed Country Work for the title track of his award-winning *Hat Town* album.

This album, which **e**____________________ new ground for Lee in terms of its content and its appeal in the contemporary charts, continues to do well for him after spawning four singles and there's still one or two songs left which have the **f**____________________ to also do very well for him on the country charts.

Bob Anthony in *Country Update* magazine, Issue 18

2 Underline the correct answer. This passage tells us all about Kernaghan's:

a album *Hat Town* **b** Kernaghan's recognition as a country music star

3 Underline the correct answer. All the paragraphs deal with:

a some aspect of Kernaghan's rise to fame **b** another development in his music

4 Underline the correct alternative. Because we know a music review is concerned with the music rather than with the performer as a person, we can say this piece of writing is a music review/a celebrity report.

Word usage

Metaphors are used by all good writers (not just poets—see Chapter 7). A **metaphor** is a comparison which is so close that the comparison become the description, e.g.

Mr Browne was a new broom in our classroom. In less than five minutes, he had us stop talking, sit up straight and listen as we had never done for any other teacher.

1 Underline the metaphors in the following.

a The Murphys and the Hardys went to war over the height of their dividing fence.

b 'John's a Kenworth, not an Alfa Romeo Sports, if you get my meaning,' Ted told Ian.

2 Reread the passage 'Hitmaker of the Decade' and then do the following:

a Write the farming metaphor used in the last paragraph: ______________________

b Explain what is meant by the metaphor *spawning four singles*.

____

3 Underline each metaphor and all the words that extend it in the following.

Elizabeth sowed the seeds of discontent among her neighbours. She watered them daily with visits to each woman during which she remarked how strongly Mrs So-and-So felt and was rewarded finally with a harvest beyond her wildest expectations—a whole street demonstration outside the council chambers demanding Rose Street be closed to heavy trucks.

Quick think

Can you find words based on the Latin words *ambulo* (I walk), *laboro* (I work) and *porto* (I carry) to mean the following?

1 to walk in a leisurely fashion ______________

2 a conveyance for the injured ______________

3 Mines in Australia pay their __________ very high wages.

4 Patients can be described as either stretcher cases or ______________ patients.

5 able to be carried ______________

6 It's not fair. You go swimming and I __________ away completing this assignment.

7 the carrying of a boat overland from one river to the next ______________

8 one who carries luggage ______________

9 Shearing sheep is __________ work.

10 Science experiments in a __________ must be carefully and safely conducted.

Proofreading

Correct the usage and spelling.

Because she was board of watching football Sally went outside, even thouh her mother reminded her it was very cold. 'I'm more tolerant to cold than you think, Mum,' she laughed. 'I'm not a potencial 'flu victim. You and Dad have this expection that I'll pick up a cold every time the tempreture drops below 25 degrees.'

Idiom

Explain:

1 When he gets back from detention I bet he'll be singing a different tune. ______________________

____

2 To my surprise, Peta was a now show at the party. ______________________

____

Writing paragraphs and whole texts

1 Number these in paragraph order to form a plan for a review of a new album.

a Likely market for this album _____

b Recommendation to buy this album _____

c Musical highlights of this album _____

d General comment about appeal of album _____

e Background account of singer's achievements to date _____

2 Choose your favourite singer or group. Write two paragraphs reviewing what you consider their best album and explaining why you think people should buy it.

Paragraph 1. Include the name of the artist and the name of the album, and what it is like in comparison to earlier materials by that artist.

Paragraph 2. Describe the best features of this new album. Refer to particular tracks that you like and explain why they appeal to you. Suggest what other people may also like.

____

____

____

____

____

____

____

____

____

____

____

3 Choose two songs by your favourite singer/group. In two paragraphs explain why you prefer one to the other. In paragraph 1 include what you like most in the first work (voice, lyrics, style of delivery, melody etc.). In paragraph 2 include any similarities between the second and the first work, then the differences between the two. Point out what it is especially that makes this the better piece.

Chapter test

1 Is the word *contemporary* used correctly in this sentence? Yes/No

I like nothing better than to listen to contemporary music by Bach and Beethoven.

2 Which sentence is correct? a __ or b __ ?

a I'm bored of watching DVDs all day. Let's go outside and play cricket.

b I'm bored with watching DVDs all day. Let's go outside and play cricket.

3 What punctuation mark is missing at point **x**?

i a colon **ii** a dash **iii** a comma

When he entered the teacher asked**x** 'Where have you been, Peter?'

4 Circle the correct answer. This sentence is an extended:

a comparison **b** metaphor **c** simile

The music flowed gently, suddenly picked up speed and crashed over rocks of clashing cymbals and deep bass notes till finally settling into a placid lake of violin reverie.

CHAPTER 12

Radio advertisement

STRUCTURE

- *dialogue format*
- *written as text for listening only*
- *background context important*

attention-getting introduction

scene-setting text and background effects

the climax/point of advertisement

Speaker A: Hey, with a Hoyts movie passport we could win a trip to L.A.!

Speaker B: AAAWWWicked!!

Speaker A: Imagine it, man—you an' me … in L.A. Free entry to Disneyland Universal Studios, I'd cruise the Boulevard and Sunset Strip. What would you do if you won?

Speaker B: I'd probably take my girlfriend.

Music

Speaker C: See a movie today at Hoyts, Belconnen, to get a movie passport and you could win a trip for two to L.A. plus great movie discount passes. Hoyts have all the best new movies these school holidays, so get down there. It's all happening at Hoyts—entertainment to the max!

Radio 1053.2CA

LANGUAGE FEATURES

- *chosen with an ear to the effect on a listener*

suggests excited delivery

colloquialism targeted to market (teenagers)

humorous anticlimax to excitement

factual instruction

inducement

disguised point of advertisement

return to hyped-up excitement in colloquialism

Comprehension

1 Underline the correct answer. This advertisement is trying to sell:

a a movie passport **b** a trip to L.A.

c movie tickets **d** discounted movie passes

2 Underline the correct answer. This advertisement's target audience is:

a teenagers **b** school students

c young employed people **d** senior primary students

3 In what country are Sunset Strip and the Boulevard? ______________________

4 Underline the best answer in the context of the advertisement. Speakers A and B are:

a boyfriend and girlfriend **b** two boys **c** two best mates

5 At what time of year was this advertisement broadcast? ______________________

6 Underline the correct answer. You acquire a movie passport:

a by ringing the radio station **b** by visiting Universal Studios, Belconnen

c by buying a Hoyts movie ticket at Belconnen

7 Radio advertisements are often accompanied by memorable jingles. Can you explain why?

____

____

Writing skills

1 Underline the correct answer. The first line of this advertisement is:

a a statement **b** an exclamation **c** a question

2 The main selling line (key sentence/phrase) of this advertisement is:

____

3 Underline all correct answers. How would you describe the language of speakers A and B?

a formal **b** informal **c** colloquial **d** containing jargon

4 Underline the correct answer. *Wicked* in this advertisement means:

a **i** fantastic **ii** evil **iii** not to be believed

b Find another example in the advertisement of a word being used so that it means something other than its formal meaning. ______________

5 What does the script writer use to indicate pauses in speech? ______________

6 The conversation of speakers A and B is all about mates doing things together. Can you explain then the point of speaker B's last line? ______________

7 What is the purpose of the music break in the script? ______________

8 Underline all appropriate answers. The dialogue for speakers A and B is meant to:

a enthuse **b** challenge **c** provoke **d** persuade

e inform **f** command **g** argue **h** recommend

9 List three ways in which the language of the third speaker differs from the language of the first two.

______________ ______________ ______________

10 In what way is the last line of the advertisement a connection with the dialogue that preceded the music break? ______________

11 The script directions include the word *Music* after the A and B exchange for a reason. Which of the following reasons is the most important? Explain your choice.

a to add interest

b to separate the two parts of the advertisement

c to herald the introduction of essential information

Vocabulary

broadcast	**intonation**	**commercial**	**rhetorical**	**advertisement**
comparison	**targeted**	**assertion**	**niche**	**claim**

These words are all associated with broadcast advertising. They are terms you will use often in the coming years, so learn to spell and use them accurately now. Words with doubled letters can be a worry. Say them clearly and in most cases you will hear the two letters as in *com+ mercial*. *Targeted* has only one 't' because we have simply added the suffix *~ed* to the word *target*.

Focus on punctuation

Apostrophes of abbreviation & possession

If necessary look back to Chapter 3 for apostrophes of possession and to Chapter 9 for apostrophes of abbreviation.

1 Abbreviate the following using an apostrophe.

a cannot ______________________ **b** would not ______________________

c will not ______________________ **d** has not ______________________

e have not ______________________ **f** are not ______________________

2 Make the following words or phrases indicate possession with apostrophes.

a announcer ______________________ **b** sponsor ______________________

c disc jockey ______________________ **d** boys ______________________

e sailors ______________________ **f** mechanics ______________________

g cattles horns ______________________ **h** 1000 sheeps fleeces ______________________

i all fishs fins ______________________

3 Insert apostrophes where appropriate.

a Commercial radios existence depends on the amount of advertising it can attract.

b Triple Js success in recent years has been its ability to meet the youth market.

c 'We cant all be TV stars,' Michaels father told him.

d 'Well be getting married in St Marks, Darling Point,' the soap star told the press.

e 'Were happy little Vegemites' is Australias most successful advertising jingle.

f Australian cricketers baggy green caps are known all over the world.

Select a word

Write the verbs formed from these nouns.

1 assertion ______________________ **2** broadcast ______________________

3 intonation ______________________ **4** advertisement ______________________

5 visualisation ______________________ **6** production ______________________

Grammar

Personal pronouns

Personal pronouns are small words that take the place of a noun referring to creatures and sometimes objects. They are:
I, me, my; you, your, yours; he, she, it; his, her, its; we, us, our; they, them, their.
e.g. *Elise told her parents she was going skating with their neighbours.*

1 Underline the personal pronouns.

a His uncle told them to surf between the flags.

b The band lost all its equipment in the accident.

c 'Your guitar is not here!' yelled his friend.

d Salesmen spruiking their wares on TV irritate my family intensely.

e Her advertisement for the dog did not state that it was a Great Dane

2 Rewrite the following, replacing nouns with personal pronouns wherever possible.

a Kristin invited John and all John's friends to a video-veg-out night.

____

b 'Pete's nicked me spikes,' the footballer grumbled.

____

c Sharon wanted to turn the heater off but couldn't find the heater's 'off' switch.

____

d The road sign was bright green and the sign said: 'Go back. Wrong way.'

____

e Tabitha-cat chased a mouse into the kitchen where the mouse ran under the fridge leaving Tabitha-cat lying on Tabitha's belly and whining as only a thwarted cat can.

____

____

3 Circle the noun to which the underlined pronoun refers.

a For many advertising agencies one popular jingle establishes <u>their</u> advertising credentials.

b In <u>its</u> efforts to escape the glare of the film studio the small dog hid in a costume box.

c Although <u>his</u> father is a surgeon, Hari does not want to follow in paternal footsteps but rather wants to become a professional soccer player.

d When good people give their word on something <u>it</u> can be trusted.

e The director of the musical *Hello Dolly*, being produced locally, has been confined to <u>her</u> bed with the flu.

4 Insert the appropriate personal pronoun in each space.

a The scouts could not light a fire because all ________wood was wet.

b Every possum mother carries _______baby on her back as soon as ______is too big for ______ pouch.

c The lioness licked ________ lips. Lunch for herself and ______ cubs was just walking by.

d Firemen must be very conscious of __________ own safety even while _______ fight someone else's house fire.

e Harvey whined to himself, 'That bone's ___________.That dog next door is not only _______ worst enemy; ______ is the greediest dog in the street.'

Word study

1 Insert the appropriate word from the vocabulary list in the following.

a FM radio advertisements are ________________________ at the youth market.

b The ABC charter does not allow it to ________________________ advertisements.

c The timing of a radio advertisement is a ________________________ decision.

d ________________________ between Brand X and a named product is a common strategy.

e A statement without supporting evidence is simply an ________________________.

f Grandparents are a ________________________ market for advertisers of children's products.

g Advertisers cannot make an untrue ________________________ about a product's qualities.

h The speaker's ________________________ in an ad for a hard rock CD would differ from that for a classical CD.

i 'Are you tired? Run down?' This ______________________ question is common in health advertisements.

j The purpose of an ______________________ is to sell a product.

2 Unscramble these words from the list.

a THORALICE ________________ **b** TTEGREDA ________________

c OSNRMOCPAI ________________ **d** CLAIMOMERC ________________

e TSIERENTVEDAM ________________ **f** ECHIN ________________

3 Using the prefixes *pre~*, *post~*, *anti~*, *mid~*, *fore~* make words meaning:

a the front part of the skull ______________________

b given after death (e.g. an award) ______________________

c noon ______________________

d drugs to cure bacterial infection ______________________

e a substance to reverse the effects of a poison ______________________

f a similar event that has occurred in the past ______________________

4 **a** Circle the word that is **not** a synonym for the word *niche*.

i nook **ii** cranny **iii** recess **iv** chasm

b Which word is an antonym of the word *commercial*?

i mercantile **ii** business-related **iii** donated **iv** trading

c Apart from radio waves, what else can be broadcast from the list below?

i television images **ii** seed grain **iii** sculptures **iv** aircraft control advice

5 Which question is a rhetorical question?

a 'What is your name?' asked the postman.

b 'Why does the giraffe have a long neck?' a child was heard to ask his mother.

c Madge was disgusted. 'Why does it always rain just when I want to go swimming?'

Evaluating other people's writing

Guinea pigs for sale

Females $10 each

Five adorable little balls of fluff
There are three females and two males
Mother sable, father black and sable
Four babies sable with white markings
Fifth black with white markings

Ring Sam in
Hope Street Marrickville

This advertisement will not sell the baby guinea pigs.

1 Is there a phone number included? __________

2 Could the buyer find the address? If not, why not? ____

____

3 What unnecessary information is included in the advertisement?

____

4 Sam tells us in detail about the colours of the guinea pigs and how many there are. What doesn't he tell a prospective buyer? ____

5 The advertisement includes a price. What is wrong with that price? ____

____

6 Explain why you would find this an effective or an ineffective advertisement.

____

Word usage

Always be careful that you select the past participle of the verb that belongs to it and not the past participle that belongs to another verb, e.g. the verbs *buy* and *bring* have similar past participles (*bought* and *brought*).

- The verbs *lie* and *lay* have entirely different meanings but their past tenses are often mistaken.

  LEARN: *lie—lay (I need to lie down.* [present] *I lay down yesterday.* [past])
  lay—laid (Ducks lay large eggs. The chook laid an egg.)

- Similarly, beware of words that are related in meaning but refer to different aspects of that meaning, e.g. *imply* and *infer*. LEARN: *I imply. You infer.*

1 Underline the correct alternative.

a Marj brought/bought the *Star Wars* soundtrack.
b Are you inferring/implying that I cheated you?
c Oscar's pet goanna lay/laid asleep in the sun.
d Bathroom windows are transparent/translucent.
e Cameron revealed a real flare/flair for acting.

2 Insert an appropriate word for the following list:

transparent, translucent, lay, laid, implied, inferred, flair, flare, bought, brought

a I ____________________ from his manner that he was cheating.
b Windscreens must be completely ____________________ for safety's sake.
c Amethysts are ____________________ gems.
d The hen ____________________ a warm brown egg.
e Non-swimmers ____________________ asleep in the sand on the beach.
f Fiona put the ice-creams she'd ____________________ in the esky Carmen had ____________________ with her.
g The crew of the damaged yacht sent up a distress ____________________.
h John Williamson has a real ____________________ for catching the spirit of Australia in his songs.

Quick think

1 These phrases have been borrowed from other languages into English. Can you fit them correctly in the following sentences?

in flagrante, magnum opus, ipso facto, fait accompli, in extremis

- **a** Harrison could not refuse permission because it was a ______________________________ (had already been done).
- **b** He was caught ______________________________ (in the act).
- **c** Samuel Johnson wrote many things but his dictionary was his ____________________ (great work).
- **d** That fellow stole my cricket bat ______________________________ (because of that fact) he is a thief.
- **e** The cholera victim is ______________________________ (dying).

2 Match these words to their meanings on the left.

a	persuasion	**i**	tell someone to do, think or be something without argument
b	specify	**ii**	appealing to prejudice or manipulating truth
c	dictate	**iii**	an extended advertisement presented as information
d	propaganda	**iv**	language to encourage one to act or think in a particular way
e	infomercial	**v**	to name individual facts, conditions, needs etc.

Proofreading

1 Correct the spelling and punctuation.

Radio advertisements unlike television advertisements rarely address children. this arm of the media aims comercials at teenagers and adults the reason is simpl children do not lisen to radio untill they are old enuff to apreciate pop music.

2 Correct any pronouns that are incorrect.

Fatimah and Felicity planned her excursion to the zoo very carefully. They would catch the train to Circular Quay and then a ferry to Taronga. As it turned out they just missed one. It was hauling in her gangplanks as they reached the wharf. She decided to sit and watch the buskers playing his various instruments on the Quay until another ferry arrived.

Idiom

Explain:

1 In the gym Dad is a square peg in a round hole. ______________________________

____

2 That excuse is wearing a bit thin. ______________________________

____

Writing paragraphs and whole texts

1 Which of these elements of radio advertising would help sell a new brand of jeans to a teenage market? Tick the elements you select. Then explain why the other elements would be unsuitable.

- **a** a soothing adult male voice
- **b** a careful explanation of the cut and fabric of the jeans

c dance party music as background

d several youthful excited voices talking

e a reflective flute solo background

f a recommendation from a young sports or TV soap star about the product's comfort and style

____

____

2 Choose any radio advertisement you have heard recently.

a Write down the main selling line. ______________________

b Write down the target audience. ______________________

c Describe the voice of the advertisement. ______________________

d How does the language of the advertisement appeal to its target market? (Consider the words and phrases used: colloqialisms, jargon etc.) ______________________

e If music and/or humour are part of the advertisement, explain how they make the advertisement more effective. ______________________

____

3 Choose one of the products listed below. Write a radio advertisement to sell this product. Include text of advertisement, directions for the voice delivery of the advertisement's spokesperson, directions for background, e.g. music, jingle, sound effects.

a tickets for the latest blockbuster movie (your choice)

b a video game called Cavern

c a mobile phone with a visual screen so you can see the person speaking to you

d a mistreated pony that needs a good home and is currently being cared for by the RSPCA.

____

____

____

____

____

____

____

Chapter test

1 Circle the misspelt word in this sentence.

Lisa targetted the bull's eye with her bow and arrow but the arrow fell short.

2 Write an appropriate personal pronoun in the space.

The advertising agency failed to include a sales address in ________ sales promotion.

3 Mark ✗ wherever there should be an apostrophe in this sentence.

The captain knew that his teams morale was crushed by their opponents height and bulk.

4 Circle the correct alternative.

Sally laid/lay down in the grass to watch the butterflies flit about the wildflowers.

13
CHAPTER

Magazine article

STRUCTURE

purpose: to entertain and/or inform

attention-grabbing title (in this case a song title)

introduction plus capitalised topic sentence containing core theme

body of article: A the expense

B the parents

C the children

conclusion: succinct

LANGUAGE FEATURES

rhetorical question and answer expected to be shared by readers

contrast

quotation adds authority to claim of absurd expense

writer doesn't say expense is mad; allows Watts to say it for her

carefully chosen adjectives

concise, definitive descriptions

italics indicate children's thought and speech

strong adverbs convey a lot of meaning

Send in the clowns

CHILDREN'S PARTIES HAVE CHANGED. 'What happened to the days of pin the tail on the donkey, a few cupcakes and some fairy bread?' asks David Pinder, who entertains at Melbourne birthdays dressed as a wizard. 'Years ago' says Paul Vallario, who rents out jumping castles in Sydney, 'we were lucky to get a game of cowboys and Indians and a chocolate cake.'

No-frills birthdays (eight or ten friends, sausage rolls heated by Mum, games organised by Dad) haven't died out altogether, but the trend in affluent Australian suburbia is to invite everyone in the class, phone the caterer and send in the clowns. At the Born to Party store on Sydney's lower North Shore, Manager Shannon Watts says her customers 'have one, sometimes two, entertainers, depending on the number of children. They might have a jumping castle and mobile farm as well.'

Parties such as these aren't just carefully planned, they're colour coordinated. The invitations team with paper napkins and plates, which match the banners and balloons.

'I think it's almost like a competition between the mothers,' says Watts. 'They like it to look artistic. They like to show that they've put a lot of thought into the party ... One of our customers came in and spent about $700 on decorations and lolly bags and things like that for her child's first birthday. Incredible.'

Understandably, in this climate of lavish spending and obsessive attention to detail, many parents are daunted by the prospect of hosting a party for young Isabella or Alexander. 'Mothers and fathers come in here and they're really uptight,' reports Watts. 'They get people like us to do everything for them. We organise the cakes, we do their balloons, we make their lolly bags. We walk them through the whole thing'.

Still, they get jittery on the day. 'Some people are just so wound up.' marvels David Pinder. 'They've got every child in the class and they're really stressed because it's such a big deal ... I say to them, 'Maybe next year, you'll invite ten.'

Tall and thin, with an animated face and a ring in his nose, Pinder has just finished his first gig of the weekend, a three-year-old's party in St Kilda. 'Hello everyone! I'm Wally the Wizard,' he announced when he arrived in his silky red suit, purple cape and big black boots. With few exceptions, the guests looked at him blankly: *Wizard? What's 'wizard'?*

Toddlers are a notoriously tricky audience—can't sit still, only a vague idea of what's happening—but seven- and eight-year-old boys are the ones who send shivers down party entertainers' spines. 'Little buggers,' says Pinder, recalling a party at which he threatened to turn a few of them into frogs. *Oh, yeah*? they taunted him. *Go ahead.*

'I said "Okay. Hang on a minute, I can remember the spell to turn you into a frog, but I can't remember the spell to turn you back into a little boy. What do you reckon? Will we give it a shot?"'

The boys thought not.

Jane Cadzow in *Good Weekend*, the *Sydney Morning Herald* magazine

Comprehension

1 Underline the correct answer. David Pinder is:

a an entertainer **b** a clown **c** a parent **d** a party organiser

2 Old style birthday parties were:

a complex **b** sophisticated **c** simple **d** boring affairs

3 Underline the correct answer. *Affluent Australian suburbia* is:

a the suburbs **b** the wealthy inner city **c** the city **d** the wealthy suburbs

4 Give one example of what is referred to as *obsessive attention to detail.* ______________________________

5 Wally the Wizard is always an immediate hit at parties. Is this true or false?

____

6 Party entertainers find two groups difficult audiences. Which ones?

____________________________ and ____________________________

7 According to Cadzow the expense of today's parties is caused by:

____

Writing skills

1 Underline two accurate answers. The first sentence is written in capitals to:

a mark the beginning **b** launch the discussion of the issues in the article

c summarise the theme of the article **d** catch the reader's eye

2 Why does the writer include two quotations from entertainers in paragraph one?

____

3 Insert the missing word. Cadzow q _ _ _ _ _ Pinder with the *cupcakes and fairy bread* reference.

4 How does Cadzow demonstrate that the party business is not a local phenomenon?

____

5 Insert the missing words. In paragraph 2 Cadzow _________________________ two kinds of party to _________________________ her point that change has occurred.

6 Underline the correct answer. The term *colour coordinated* as used in the passage conveys the writer's:

a approval **b** disapproval **c** sense of style **d** mocking disapproval

7 Underline any incorrect answers. The frequent use of quotations in this article:

a makes it believable **b** is the technique of a lazy writer

c indicates the nature of the party business **d** is a good space-filler

e offers interesting sidelights on the main argument of party change

8 The word *gig* is an entertainment-industry word meaning here:

a silly activity **b** paid employment **c** a musical engagement **d** a show

9 The use of the word *gig* adds a feeling of ________________________ to the article. (Select from the words: humour, authenticity, theatricality, familiarity)

10 What verb towards the end tells us that the boys were provoking Pinder by teasing and annoying him?

____

11 Underline two answers. The tone of this excerpt is:

a serious **b** light **c** humorous **d** hilarious

12 Underline the correct answer. The purpose of this writing is to:

a entertain **b** inform **c** instruct **d** describe **e** inform and entertain **f** question

Vocabulary

affluent	**daunted**	**suburbia**	**taunted**	**coordinated**
threaten	**lavish**	**recall**	**obsessive**	**vague**

These are all useful words for your own writing. By this stage you should be keeping a notebook of useful words and phrases as your own writing resource. When learning to spell them take special note of the word *obsessive*. Like the words *embarrassed* and *parallel* it is often misspelt.

Focus on punctuation

Inverted commas: revision

Remember: Use inverted commas for direct speech, quotations, titles and references.

1 Insert inverted commas where necessary.

a The refrain Who'll come a-waltzing Matilda with me is widely recognised.

b I read Winton's Blue Boy over Christmas.

c The way Elaine says Oh, my dear! is most annoying.

d Nobody in Year 8 enjoyed Davison's Man-shy but everyone thought Gleitzman's Two Weeks with the Queen hilarious.

e Richard Lovelace's line: Stone walls do not a prison make is a famous quotation.

f For the love of Mike! Put things away when you're finished with them! roared his brother.

2 Punctuate with appropriate inverted commas.

a The death of the tiger shark in Winton's Blue Boy was the saddest thing I have ever read, Benni confided to his mate.

b Do you think I'd make a good clown—Hey there, kiddies, I'm Clarrie the clown—well, what do you think, Lisa? Toby asked his sister.

Select a word

1 Write synonyms for *funny*.

a h _ _ _ r _ _ _ **b** a _ _ _ _ _ g **c** h _ l _ _ _ _ _ _ **d** up _ _ _ r _ _ _ s

2 Write homonyms for these words.

a peer ________________ (a jetty) **b** ascent ________________ (agreement)

c medal ________________ (to interfere) **d** gorilla ________________ (a fighter)

Grammar

Nouns: concrete, abstract, proper

Nouns name things.

- **Common nouns** name everything in our environment, e.g. *tree, house, sky, dog, boy, parent, steel, shed, ship, flower, book.*

  Common nouns can be:
  Concrete—naming things we can see feel, taste and touch, e.g. *desk, tree, bird, ocean*
  Abstract—naming intangible things (things we can't see or touch), e.g. *anger, anxiety, happiness, concentration, loneliness*

- **Proper nouns** are the special names that identify individual people, places and things, e.g. *James, Australia, Parliament.*

1 Underline all proper nouns and circle all concrete nouns.

a 'Fingerlings are fish the size of your little finger,' the Inspector of Fisheries scolded the poacher.

b The great success of Peter Jackson's Ring films was the combination of live film with animation.

c In early Sydney habitual criminals were sent to Norfolk Island.

d Henry Parkes introduced public education in New South Wales in 1870.

e Australia's Ian McDougall leads the world in ocean temperatures research.

2 Underline any abstract noun in the following.

a Addiction to cigarette smoking leads to lung cancer.

b His concern for his mate sent him back to search for the boy.

c Accident victims can suffer distress for years afterwards.

d Education is the aspiration of anyone who wants to get ahead in the world.

e His eyes widened in terror at the thought of something slimy crawling up his back.

3 Convert these adjectives to abstract nouns.

a savage ____________________ **b** weary ____________________

c kind ____________________ **d** ambitious ____________________

e amiable ____________________ **f** valuable ____________________

4 Convert these verbs to abstract nouns.

a suspect ____________________ **b** avenge ____________________

d intend ____________________ **d** irritate ____________________

e accelerate ____________________ **f** believe ____________________

Word study

1 Match a word from the vocabulary list to the following:

a uncertain or unclear ____________________

b extravagant ____________________

c discouraged or intimidated ____________________

d wealthy ____________________

2 Insert an appropriate word from the vocabulary list.

a Do you ________________________ the words of 'The Man From Snowy River'?

b Those black clouds ________________________ the staging of our outdoor concert.

c My next-door neighbour is ________________________ about keeping her lawn weed-free.

d Our last school social was ________________________ in colours of purple and gold.

3 Make nouns of the following.

a recollect ________________________ **b** affluent ________________________

c obsessive ________________________ **d** coordinated ________________________

e threaten ________________________ **f** taunted ________________________

4 Write antonyms for the following.

a affluence p _ _ _ _ _ y **b** lavish m _ _ g re

c threaten enc _ _ r _ g _ **d** vague c _ _ _ _ _ n

5 Write a list word in each of the spaces.

a His ______________ lifestyle is characterised by fast cars, yachts and business jets.

b Most inner cities are surrounded by a ______________ of small houses and backyards.

c Oscar looked ______________ when I asked him if he'd seen my bat. 'Maybe in the shed,' he muttered.

d The bully ____________ the smallest boy in the class until we all stopped him.

Word usage

1 **a** Insert these words correctly in the blanks in the following article.

hierarchical, kneeling, unique, savagely, relocated, isolation

Young hooligans

Culling operations in Kruger National Park, South Africa, have produced a **i** ____________________________ problem. In 1994 rangers in other national parks began finding **ii** ____________________________ wounded white rhinos dead at the rate of about one a month. Poachers were at first suspected but the truth when discovered was macabre. The rhinos had been murdered but the perpetrators were elephants—young aggressive bull elephants that did in the rhinos by knocking them over, **iii** ____________________________ on them and goring them.

The trouble-making elephants are all orphans **iv** ____________________________ to other parks after Kruger culling operations. Since 1978 almost 1500 orphan calves, 600 of them male, have thus been raised with no exposure to adult elephants or to the **v** ____________________________ structure that defines an elephant's life.

The long-term effect of this **vi** ____________________________ from adult supervision appears to be a generation of juvenile delinquents.

Adapted from an article by Michael D. Lemonick in *Time* magazine

b Underline the two topic sentences and circle the key word in each topic sentence.

c In one sentence explain why the young elephants behave in this murderous fashion.

____

d **i** In the article find a colloquial expression meaning *murdered* ______________________ and a word meaning *gruesome* ______________________ .

ii Complete the following: *Young hooligans* and *juvenile delinquents* are descriptions usually applied to

____

iii Insert the missing letters. In this passage these terms are used m _ t _ p h _ _ _ _ _ _ ly.

2 A magazine article on a controversial topic must be seen to even-handed. Here are some words and phrases that help to achieve this.

however, nevertheless, on the contrary, on the other hand, it could be said, the fact that, even though, generally speaking, as a rule

Insert one of the words or phrases above in each of the spaces.

> Australian wildlife, ______________________, has suffered greatly since European settlement. ______________ in recent years people have taken steps to protect our native creatures, many still die as a result of our ignorance and our carelessness. ____________, it is not all bad news on the wild front. Control of the rabbit population has allowed many species of lizard and the bilby to come back from the brink. ________________, feral cats now pose as great a threat to wild creatures as rabbits once did.

3 **Homonyms** are words that sound the same but mean different things.

- Where = place (Remember: H for *home.*)
- Wear = be clothed in (Remember: A for *armband* worn as a sign of mourning.)
- We're = we are (Remember: ' = a.)

Insert where/we're/wear as appropriate.

a Although we're listed for canteen duty __________________ not required.

b Quartz country is __________________ gold is likely to be found.

c Cats prowled __________________ fish were unloaded on the dock.

d We will all __________________ silly hats for New Year's Eve.

e __________________ going to explore the Kruger National Park.

4 • Your = ownership • You're = you are • Yore = ancient times

Insert your/you're/yore as appropriate.

a In days of __________________ court clowns were called jesters.

b '__________________ a little beauty!' Rex declared, kissing his catch.

c '__________________ not really a clown,' the obnoxious child announced.

d '__________________ pants are too big,' laughed the toddler at the clown.

e 'Will you lend me __________________ make-up?' whispered one clown to the other.

Quick think

1 Humour has many forms. Can you identify these forms of humour popularised by clowns and comedians and script writers?

a pie-in-the-face, slip-on-a-banana-skin humour: s _ _ _ s t _ _ k humour

b humour where the situation involved is usually considered tragic: b _ _ _ k humour

c humour which shows up the faults of people and institutions usually considered above criticism: s _ t _ re

d humour in ordinary everyday situations: s _ t _ _ tion comedy

2 Parties are celebratory gatherings. Match these other gatherings to their descriptions.

a	wake	**i**	a small evening gathering of those interested in music or literature
b	testimonial	**ii**	a dinner and dance evening in formal dress
c	soiree	**iii**	dinner in honour of someone who has made a great contribution to life
d	black tie ball	**iv**	a post-funeral celebration of the life of the deceased

Proofreading

Correct spelling and usage (look for incorrect homonyms).

Not coming from afluant suberbia Kenny spent much of his holidays down on the key, fishing. His fishing storey tonight was hilarous.

'Your never going to belive this. I cort a seagul. It swooped in and swollowed a little brim just as I was realing it in. Took me twenty minuts to get the hook and line out of the stupid bird. And now I'm wering everything he eight since he got up this morning!'

Idiom

Explain:

1 That would never happen in <u>a month of Sundays</u>. ______________________

____

2 <u>'I wouldn't touch it with a bargepole,'</u> Henry declared as he eyed the pile of rotting rubbish.

____

Writing paragraphs and whole texts

1 Mark these topics M or N as suitable for a magazine article or a newspaper item of news.

a 5 pm traffic jam on the Sydney Harbour Bridge today _____

b Poisonous creatures of our coastline _____

c Youth and the cyberscene _____

d Minister says Olympics on Track _____

e Alex the whale frolics off Bondi _____

f Gentle giants of the sea—a conservation success story _____

2 You are writing magazine articles on the following subjects.

a The perils of going to the beach

b The lack of youth facilities in the suburbs

c A school with students from 29 countries

d Romance—nineties style

Write an eye-catching title and an explanatory subtitle for each. For example, an article about a successful school with students from 29 countries could be headed:

Twenty-nine Ways to Say Hello

Barnley H.S.—a Model for Australia

3 Write an <u>introductory</u> paragraph for an article about brand-name clothing and why parents and teenagers have different opinions on the subject. Use one of these topic sentences:

a Brand-name clothing keeps families at war.

b The issue of brand-name clothing divides the generations.

4 Finish a concluding paragraph about the perils of public transport, beginning with *Home at last!*

5 Draw up a plan for an article about the effectiveness of school sport in promoting teenage exercise. Use the framework below.

- Paragraph 1—introduction. State your main idea about the subject.
- Paragraphs 2, 3 and 4—the body of your article. Give one example in each paragraph to support your case for or against its effectiveness.
- Paragraph 5—conclusion. Restate you main idea and sum up your case. Invent an interesting closing sentence.

Chapter test

1 Circle the correct alternative.
The affluence/effluence of some countries is obvious in the number of air conditioners they use.

2 The underlined noun is an abstract noun. True/False
The Temperature falls as a plane climbs and reaches high altitudes.

3 Which sentence is correctly punctuated?
a Jawaharlal Nehru was a Prime Minister of India Mr Harvey told us.
b Jawaharlal Nehru was a prime minister of India Mr Harvey told us.
c 'Jawaharlal Nehru was a Prime Minister of India,' Mr Harvey told us.
d 'Jawaharlal Nehru was a Prime Minister of India' Mr Harvey told us.

4 Circle the correct alternative
May I borrow you're/your drama notes, please?

CHAPTER 14

Classified advertisement

STRUCTURE

purpose: to inform/sell

main point to be known/sold

details:
- *selling points*
- *information about main point*

price/ conditions advertiser contact details

A LOST/KELPIE X SHEPHERD. M. 6yo. black/tan/cream, red collar and tags. Gosford area 10/8. Reward 6293 3184	**B JEEP** Cherokee Sports. 94. 68 000 km. excel. cond. $27,500. ENK218 Ph. 7008 9273
C CANINE TRAINING COLLEGE Basic obedience, on-off lead, Personal Protection, guard, security. At your home or board-training 1800 647 651 or 9894 1244. All work guaranteed or no fee.	**D RACEHORSE GELDING** This horse has had one win, 5 placings & is racing in 2 weeks. Quarter share—$12,000, $300 pw will cover all costs, no extras. (08) 4532 7963
E Midnight Waters Blue Water Charters 'The Albatross' Tuna and reef fishing. All gear and bait supplied. Fast modern boat. Midweek Discounts—Reef & Game. Free call: 1800 248 561 ozemail.com.au/mnightcharters	**F ANTIQUES** We have 4 showrooms of Victorian, Edwardian and 1920s furniture. Large selection always available. Also good range of porcelain, silver, crystal and collectables. Open 7 Days, 6 Barrabogie Street, Halston. Ph: 5439 3331
G JAGUAR X15.V12 coupe 1980. auto. good old jag. unreg. $6000 ono. 5930 3141.	**H Rivka's Psychic & Tarot** Future of your relationships Global Psychics. $3 /min Mob xtra 24 hrs 1904 313 066
I Bendourie/Wylie Creek area beachside homes/units, linen only reqd. Banks-Chen P/L. Lic. Agent. 4 Federation Dr. Wylie Creek Ph. (06) 4471 2244	**J NELSON** (with the funny eye) is home. Thank you everyone for your help.

LANGUAGE FEATURES

brevity, abbreviation, jargon, note-form construction, factual

auto jargon

note-form construction

antiques jargon

colloquialism to appeal to another Jaguar fan

identifying phrase: a reference to a previous lost advertisement

brief, abbreviated details—factual only

Comprehension

1 You could buy an old-style silver cutlery set at Halston. Is this true or false? ______________________

2 Underline the correct alternative. You would/would not have to take camp beds if you rented a holiday home at Bendourie.

3 Name the boat on which you could go deep sea fishing. ______________________

4 Underline the correct alternative.

The charge for a psychic reading over the phone is/is not a standard price for all calls.

5 Explain what is being sold in advertisement D. ____

____

6 What must have happened to Nelson? ______________________

7 You could drive home the Jaguar in advertisement G immediately you bought it. Is this true or false? ________

8 The jeep in advertisement B is a current model. True/False?____________

9 Advertisement C promises *All work guaranteed or no fee.* Explain clearly what this means in terms of the training of your dog. ____

____

10 The person who has placed the advertisement is the v _ _ _ _ _ and the person who wants to buy the item advertised is the buyer or p _ _ _ _ _ _ _ _ .

Writing skills

1 Underline which of the following is not possible. Advertising in the classified columns is not cheap. Therefore, the text must be:

a brief **b** fully detailed **c** abbreviated **d** condensed **e** informative

2 Insert the missing letters and word. The need for brevity means big words have to be abb _ _ _ _ _ ted, e.g. *excel. cond.* in advertisement B means ____________________.

3 In advertisement G the letters *ono* mean ____________________.

4 Underline the correct answer. An advertisement saying *ono* means:

a You pay a fixed price. **b** You can bargain the price down 50%.

c You may purchase for a price slightly less than what is asked.

5 Specialist jargon can simplify the message for specialist buyers who know what they want. Find an example of auto jargon in advertisement B ____________________.

6 In advertisement C the advertiser has offered an inducement as well as information. What phrase offers this inducement?

____

7 Advertisement E offers another kind of inducement to respond. What is it?

____

8 Insert the missing word. The X in advertisement A tells us the missing dog is a _ _ _ _ _ bred dog.

9 Insert the missing letters. The purpose of listing an advertisement in the classifieds is to reach a wider m _ _ k _ t than can be reached by word of mouth.

10 Underline the correct answer. Reread all the advertisements. After the item for sale is described, what information is the only other essential piece of information in an advertisement?

a price of item **b** address of item **c** vendor contact information **d** a guarantee

Vocabulary

guarantee	**crystal**	**guard**	**porcelain**	**charter**
discount	**available**	**collectable**	**required**	**relationship**

Underline the *gua~* spelling pattern in *guarantee* and *guard*. This causes problems for many students. Practise this pattern with such words as *guardian* and *guarantor*. Circle *crystal*. This is a common trick word in listening tests, so learn to spell it accurately. Don't forget the Look, Cover, Write, Check method.

*F*ocus on punctuation

Revision

1 Rewrite making all necessary corrections and insertions of punctuation.

'Boots, black, brown, suede, patent, all styles, all sizes.' This catalogue entry stood out among the odds and sods of the auction listing Taylor's Annual Clearing Sale listing. I turned to Gino Pirelli: our next-door neighbour: 'Fancy some old style footwear?'. He guffawed. 'Me? I wear runners mate runners with Pirelli tread on them.'

2 Tick the one that is correctly punctuated.

a **i** For sale: sun-ripened tomatoes'.
ii For sale: sun-ripened tomatoes.

b **i** They're not all here yet.
ii Theyre not all here yet.

c **i** We were'nt told the news until too late.
ii We weren't told the news until too late.

d **i** Alice's hat fell into the river.
ii Alices' hat fell into the river.

*S*elect a word

Find synonyms in the vocabulary list for the following.

1 warranty ______________________ **2** needed ______________________

3 ceramic ______________________ **4** protect ______________________

5 hire ______________________ **6** price cut ______________________

Grammar

The odd verb *to be*

- Verbs usually have a subject and an object, e.g.
  John chased the dog. John = subject; the dog = object.
  You chased me. You = subject; me = object.
- What is odd about the verb *to be* is that, if the object that follows it is a personal pronoun, it must be a nominative personal pronoun; i.e. a personal pronoun that is usually used as a subject, e.g.
  Who's there? It is I, John.
  It was he who broke the window.
- After the word *if* the form of the verb *to be* is always *were* in sentences like these:
  If I were a genius I wouldn't have to study so hard.
  I'd go swimming if it weren't so cold.
  If I were a rich man I'd drive a Porsche.

1 Following the rule above, underline the correct alternative.

a It was her/she who donated that fine shield to the competition.

b It wasn't Alisha, it was I/me who borrowed the cricket gear yesterday.

c It was my father not me/I who advertised that car for sale.

d The ladies might have caught the fish but it was us/we men who cooked it so well.

e It wasn't he/him who asked the question, I asked it.

2 Insert the correct form of the verb *to be* in the spaces.

a If I __________ a tradesman I'd like to be an electrician.

b Mitch could fix it if he __________ here.

c If Margy __________ not so sick we would be going to the beach.

d If the Principal __________ to declare a holiday we'd all cheer.

e If everyone __________ to smile, what a happy world it would be.

3 Correct the following by underlining the error and writing the correction.

a If you were me you'd have the same trouble with chemical equations. __________

b If it were him who had to decide we'll still be waiting for a decision tomorrow. __________

c If I were her I'd apply for that job. __________

d It was them who volunteered to help the disabled students. __________

Word study

1 Find a word from the vocabulary list to match the following.

a written promise that the sold item will operate without a problem for a fixed period or be fixed without cost to the buyer ____________________

b a percentage deducted from the list price ____________________

c stamps, butterflies, matchboxes, teaspoons are all examples of ____________________s.

d to hire a vehicle and its owner/driver ____________________

2 Insert an appropriate word from the vocabulary list.

a The ____________________ between Eddie and Mr Hales is that of player and coach.

b A strobe light was all that was ____________________ to complete the decor for the social.

c A dainty ____________________ figurine is one of our family's heirlooms.

d Are you ____________________ to work in Saturday's clean-up drive?

3 licence = a permit (written permission to do something)
to license = the act of giving that permission, issuing that permit

a What do the following advertisement references mean?

i *Gold lic. No. 4690* means 4690 is the number of a tradesperson's ____________________.

ii *Lics'd antique dealer* means this person is legally p _ _ m _ _ _ _ d to sell antiques.

b Underline the correct alternative. A *licensed* restaurant is one permitted to sell soft drinks/alcohol as well as meals.

4 Underline the correct alternative.

a Mr Jones is a licenced/licensed dealer in second-hand goods.

b The Pink Pig is a licensed/licenced restaurant.

c My grandfather has held a driving license/licence for forty years.

d His pilot's license/licence was cancelled after he ignored safety regulations.

e Always employ a tradesperson who holds a gold license/licence.

5 Complete these *gu*~ words

a	association of skilled workers	g u _ _ d	**b**	estimate	g u _ _ s
c	resident visitor	g u _ _ t	**d**	sense of having done wrong	g u _ _ t
e	deceit or cunning	g u _ _ e	**f**	show the way	g u _ _ e
g	old-style coin	g u _ _ _ a	**h**	fruit	g u _ v a
i	protector	g u _ _ _ _ _ n	**j**	irregular soldier	g u _ _ _ _ _ a

Evaluating other people's writing

Wanted to buy

Small car with 4 doors, registered, manual gearbox, mag wheels, first class sound system, no rust, body without dents or scratches. Willing to pay up to $2000.

1 Write appropriate abbreviations for the underlined words. ______________________________

2 Circle two words that could be deleted.

3 Underline the correct answer. Which of the following is the best concise, positive and accurate version of *no rust, body without dents or scratches*:

a rust-free, dentless **b** clean, straight **c** no rust, straight **d** immaculate

4 What is missing from this advertisement? ______________________________

5 What is unreasonable ('Tell 'im he's dreaming') about this advertisement?

____

Word usage

A **euphemism** is a phrase or a statement that avoids the hard truth of a situation. For example, instead of saying someone has died we often say he/she has *gone to a better world*. Advertisers are very good at inventing euphemisms to disguise the truth, e.g. about a worn-out sports car: *Sunday-driven by lady driver only*. (The lady was a Sunday racing competitor at the Oran Park track.)

1 Match the everyday euphemisms to their meanings:

a under the weather ________ **i** go to the toilet
b dropped off the perch ________ **ii** Alzheimer's disease
c oldtimer's disease ________ **iii** we lost
d visit the loo ________ **iv** died
e we came second ________ **v** drunk

2 Match these examples of advertising euphemisms to the real state of affairs.

a this house is a handyperson's dream ________ **i** unwanted mongrel litter
b this has the style of yesteryear ________ **ii** needs lots of repair
c six adorable x-bred pups ________ **iii** run-down inner city dwelling
d loads of potential, close to the CBD ________ **iv** very old

3 Some phrases and abbreviations occur frequently in advertisements. Match the following.

a as is, where is ________ **i** statement of employment record
b first to see will buy ________ **ii** great sense of humour
c immaculate condition ________ **iii** between the hours of 9 am and 5 pm only
d tariff ________ **iv** for sale in existing condition
e fin. sec. ________ **v** unmarked appearance
f a.h. ________ **vi** a good bargain
g bus. hrs. ________ **vii** accommodation charge
h GSOH ________ **viii** financially secure
i résumé ________ **ix** after 5 pm

Quick think

1 In car sales advertisements what do the following terms mean?

a interior trim: inside up _ _ _ s t _ _ y

b sound system: radio/CD/tape player plus two or more sp _ _ _ _ _ s

c mags: wide w _ _ _ _ _

d alloys: wheel h _ _ _ made of alloyed metal

e customised: altered to suit o _ _ er's own tastes

f mint condition: as n _ _ condition

2 Match the following real estate terms to their meanings

a	split level	**i**	the largest bedroom
b	terrace house	**ii**	wide unroofed external floor area
c	recently refurbished	**iii**	not covered by house roof, a separate building
d	master bedroom	**iv**	built on two levels, one higher than the other.
e	deck	**v**	one house in a row of houses sharing external walls.
f	duplex	**vi**	recently renovated
g	freestanding	**vii**	two houses sharing one external wall

Proofreading

Correct for spelling and tense consistency.

My Dad loves selling things through the classfieds. Every Wensday he'd be on the phone ringing the latest ad. through to the offece of our local paper. The trouble was then he'd go out on Satuday mornings.

'Just got to duck out for a few minuts'—and off he goes. He's no sooner out the door than the phone starts ringing.

'My Dad's not availible just now. He'll be back hear in half an hour.'

When he's not back by eleven that's when I usally start selling things for whatever the caller wants to pay.

When he got back ('Cort talking to Fred Pearce') he'd always be satified with the dele I'd done. He tells me I shood be a salsman when I leave school but he wories that one day I'll give a garantee on one of his sales and then he will regret going out on Saturdays.

Idiom

Explain:

1 I bought a red-hot bargain at Paddy's today. ______________________

____

2 This house has all mod cons. ______________________

____

Writing paragraphs and whole texts

1 Rewrite this advertisement abbreviating and omitting words wherever possible.

Handsome older Holden sedan (EH model). Has been fully restored with an excellent paint job, immaculate interior finish, rechromed trim and bumper bars. Its motor and gearbox are fully reconditioned. It is registered until July 2000. For sale for $3800 or near offer. Phone 02 6543 791 after hours.

2 You have a size 16, current style Raiders football jersey. You wish to swap it for a Nintendo Gameboy or a current hit CD. Write the advertisement for this using no more than 10 words.

3 For the Public Notices column write an advertisement for a Blue Light Disco in your town. Include date, time, location and conditions of entry.

4 Write a 2-line entry for the Wanted column seeking a small desexed dog, not necessarily pedigreed, that is tolerant of cats and small children, is house-trained and, preferably, obedience-trained. Use abbreviations and don't forget your contact details.

5 You have rescued a cat and three kittens abandoned in a garbage bin in the park. Advertise for homes for them. Make sure you include information that will make people want to adopt them.

Chapter test

1 Which sentence is correct?

a It was her that stole the library book **b** It was she who stole the library book.

2 Complete this sentence.

If it __________ my choice, I'd go and see a film.

3 Circle the correctly spelt alternative.

The vendor garanteed/guaranteed the roadworthiness of the vehicle.

4 Circle the correct alternative.

The Fisheries officer checked all the fishermen's licenses/licences.

CHAPTER 15

Factual description

The Oodnadatta Track

The Oodnadatta Track follows a chain of waterholes known as the 'string of springs', which was also an Aboriginal trade route.

Near the iron railway bridge at Algebuckina Creek, we pulled off at a waterhole several hundred metres long. 'When it's hot and we've got backpackers on board, they go skinny-dipping,' said John wistfully. 'Off with their gear and into it. Doesn't worry them a bit. Europeans!' and his voice trailed off as he put the bus into reverse, a little hurriedly I thought, lest we be tempted to follow their example.

It was dark by the time we reached William Creek. The town has a population of seven: 'But it's got a hotel, a golf course, an airport and a racetrack. What more could you ask for?' said John. The main street at William Creek doubles as a runway, and our headlights picked out two aircraft parked at the front of the pub.

The William Creek pub is an outback legend. T-shirts dangling from the ceiling commemorated the visit of Fiona from County Durham, Sven from Sweden and Alison from Dubbo. There was a camel safari in the bar—cameleers with stovepipe arms, shredded sleeves, chewed-up hats and enormous grins, plus a couple of wide-eyed American clients.

After William Creek, we stopped briefly at Anna Creek, billed as the largest cattle station on earth. Most of the afternoon we had been driving on this single property, part of the empire carved a century ago by Sir Sidney Kidman, the outback cattle baron.

It was almost 10 am by the time our wheels hit the bitumen on the outskirts of Coober Pedy. It hadn't been such a tough day after all, although my blow-up cushion hadn't survived an encounter with the rusty railway spike I'd souvenired from the track of the old Ghan.

There could have been a moral there but I was too bushed to work it out.

Extract from an article 'Desert Storm' by Michael Gebicki in *Sunday Life* magazine

STRUCTURE

- *simple factual title tells what is to be described*
- *brief introduction*
- *body of description*
  - *skinny-dipping*
  - *William Creek*
  - *the journey along the track*
- *brief conclusion*

LANGUAGE FEATURES

- *metaphor*
- *quotation is a way of letting us know about a person without actually describing him*
- *facts contrast: population versus facilities*
- *aircraft parked underlines emptiness of town*
- *imaginative way of saying: many backpackers visit W.C.*
- *vivid word-picture (image)*
- *contrast of statement with air-cushion evidence of what he had expected*
- *colloquialisms add outback flavour*

Comprehension

1 Underline the correct answer. This passage is describing:

a William Creek **b** the Oodnadatta Track **c** Anna Creek **d** people of the outback

2 This part of Australia is known only to locals. Is this true or false? ____________________

3 The harsh conditions meant Aborigines avoided this area. Is this true or false? ____________________

4 *Skinny dipping* in this article means:

a only thin people swim **b** only Europeans swim **c** swimmers are naked

5 What is the evidence for William Creek's main street being long and straight?

____

6 Insert the missing word. For most of the journey Gebicki travelled on ______________ roads.

7 Underline the correct answer. The old Ghan was:

a an elderly Afghan cameleer **b** the bridge at Algebuckina Creek

c a train **d** an off-road vehicle with metal treads

8 John, the driver, is accustomed to making this trip. Is this true or false? ______________

9 What do the words *billed as the largest cattle station on earth* mean? ______________

____

10 What Australianism does Gebicki use to describe being too tired to do another thing? ______________

____

Writing skills

1 Insert the missing letters. The writing plan for this description is based on the stages of the j _ _ _ _ _ y.

2 Insert the missing word. The mention of the ______________ lets us know Gebicki had anticipated an uncomfortable day's travelling without his actually telling us that fact.

3 Underline what does not apply. The description suggests that the outback is:

a hot **b** unpleasant **c** vast **d** fascinating **e** remote **f** unknown

4 Insert the missing letters. The writer uses the metaphor *a chain of waterholes* to c _ _ d _ _ _ e a lengthy explanation into a single image.

5 Complete the words. Listen to the phrase *a string of springs*. What poetic devices have been used here to enhance the effectiveness of the description? a _ _ _ _ _ _ _ _ _ _ _ and r _ _ _ _

6 Insert the missing letters. *Cameleers with stovepipe arms* is a colourful image designed to emph _ _ _ _ e the size of the men's arms. Such exag _ _ _ _ tion is called **hyperbole**.

7 Insert the missing word. What word tells us that the American tourists found it all a bit overwhelming and unbelievable? ______________

8 Insert the missing words. What verb summarises the hard times Sidney Kidman had establishing his great cattle empire? ______________

9 Underline the correct answer. This piece of description is:

a informative **b** entertaining **c** informative and entertaining **d** imaginative

10 The final sentence suggesting there was *a moral there* is intended to make the reader s _ _ p and t _ _ _ k about the article before turning the page.

____

Vocabulary

remote	**abandoned**	**solitary**	**isolated**	**resourceful**
commemorate	**spike**	**wistfully**	**bitumen**	**encounter**

Many words deal with the same area of meaning, but they are not identical in meaning, e.g. the first four words. Using your dictionary make sure you understand the exact meaning of each and practise using it in sentences. Underline the spelling of *commemorate*. Like *parallel* it is commonly misspelt.

Focus on punctuation

1 Insert appropriate punctuation.

a Dr Rashids surgery is adjacent to Harriss bakery.

b Where's the mail for Augathella station? asked the stockman.

c Pool rules are no running no jumping no bombing and definitely no ducking.

d Eddie likes watching ants the big red sugar ants that live under the old wattle tree.

e Where did you put my sneakers Susan asked her sister.

2 Correct the punctuation.

a 'I can't find it!' whispered the boy beside him. 'It's on Smithys' desk. Its' called 'Calculus for Fun' but its not funny.'

b The chest was full of gems, diamonds, emeralds, rubies, sapphires, even opals.

c Harry Petrecevic the carpenter has done an exceptional job restoring Foleys' Folly; that derelict shack made of beer bottles on the outskirts of Coober Pedy

d I wonder why he chose that shirt?

e We dont' know if its going to rain today

3 Write the contractions for the following:

a should not____________________ **b** will not ____________________

c did not ____________________ **d** cannot ____________________

4 Abbreviate the following for inclusion in advertisements.

a excellent condition ____________________ **b** including ____________________

c or near offer ____________________ **d** to be announced ____________________

e experienced____________________ **f** required ____________________

Select a word

Find synonyms for the following from the vocabulary list.

1 meet ____________________ **2** forsaken ____________________

3 distant ____________________ **4** capable ____________________

5 pitch or tar ____________________ **6** alone ____________________

Grammar

Revision

Be careful with verb agreement.

- Ask 'Who or what?' before the verb to decide what noun or pronoun you are fitting the verb to, e.g.

  All kinds of fruit were exhibited.
  Pl. noun Pl. verb

  This sort of thing is not to be tolerated.
  Sing. noun Sing. verb

- Determining words also give a clue to the choice of verb; *each, every, any (of these)* refer to one person or thing and so are followed by a singular verb, e.g. *Every boy is silent.*

  Some is always followed by a plural verb, e.g. *Some students were late for class.*

  Similarly the nouns *anyone, anything, everyone* and *everything* are followed by singular verbs, e.g. *Everyone is invited to Sally's party.*

1 Underline the correct alternatives.

- **a** This sort of desert snake/snakes is/are dangerous.
- **b** The crowd is/are restless.
- **c** Many makes of car/cars was/were on display
- **d** Some of the newer models have/has been custom built.
- **e** All sorts of sweets are/is included in that show bag.
- **f** Anything are/is acceptable as dress for that barbecue.
- **g** Any of these dogs is/are suitable for a family pet.
- **h** Have/Has anyone seen my purple umbrella?

2 These are revision exercises. Look back to earlier chapters if you are unsure.
Correct the following.

- **a** Can I go to the disco on Friday? ______________________
- **b** These joggers are different than those. ______________________
- **c** Neither John nor Julie eat meat. ______________________
- **d** It was him who broke the window. ______________________
- **e** I wondered weather to take my umbrella. ______________________
- **f** Brent threw the javelin right over their. ______________________

3 Insert an appropriate pronoun.

- **a** To ______________ did you lend my trumpet?
- **b** Elaine was the girl ______________ travelled overland from Adelaide to Darwin.
- **c** It was Michael Gebicki ______________ air cushion was punctured.
- **d** Anna Creek belonged to Sidney Kidman, ________was known as the Cattle King.
- **e** Sailors, __________ lives used to be fraught with danger, are safer today at sea.

4 Remove the ambiguity by writing this sentence differently.
gobbling furiously with hunger I threw wheat to the turkeys.

____

Word study

1 The following relate to words in the top row of the vocabulary list.

a Underline the correct alternative. In relation to Australia, Easter Island is/is not remote.

b Circle the solitary activity below.

i chess **ii** discussion **iii** thinking **iv** consultation

c A man avoids dying of thirst by using a flattened and funnelled drink can to direct overnight condensation into his empty water bottle. What word describes that man? ______________________

d Insert the missing word. Floodwaters ______________________ several Queensland towns for many weeks in 2011.

2 *Remember* and *commemorate* are concerned with different aspects of memory. Insert them correctly in the following.

a Lucy could ______________________ her first sight of Sydney Harbour Bridge as a toddler.

b All the town wanted to erect a plaque to ______________________ the heroism of the firefighters.

3 Insert the word *wistfully* in <u>one</u> of the following (it is correct in only one). Then select words from this list to fill the other blanks: uproariously, shyly, enthusiastically, wearily, sadly

a 'Fantastic!' Leo yelled ______________________.

b 'Do it now, not next week!' the supervisor reminded her ______________________.

c 'I wish I could go with them too', the youngest child whispered ______________________.

d Football songs are always sung ______________________.

4 The word *solitude* derives from the Latin word *solus* meaning alone. Complete these words, which have the same derivation.

a He sailed s _ _ o around the world.

b Stamp collecting like writing poetry is a s _ _ _ _ _ _ y activity.

c 'It was s _ _ _ ly my fault,' confessed Julie.

d The high point of the concert was the performance of a violin s _ _ _ ist.

Word usage

1 Using the words below, complete this commentary on Fact File.

attractions, run, written, informative, descriptive, price, facts, details, advertising, attempt, describe, trip, imagination, availability

This is **a** ______________________ but not **b** ______________________ writing. It contains many **c** ______________________ but makes no **d** ______________________ to **e** ______________________ those facts so readers can experience them in their **f** ______________________. *(continued)*

Fact File

The mail run day tour departs Coober Pedy on Tuesdays and Thursdays. The cost is $75 per person. For bookings and information, call 1800 069 911.

Coober Pedy has a wide choice of accommodation, including campgrounds, backpacker hostels and motels. The Desert Cave is the best in town, with some rooms located underground. For bookings, call 1800 291 958. Kendall Airlines has daily flights to Coober Pedy from Adelaide.

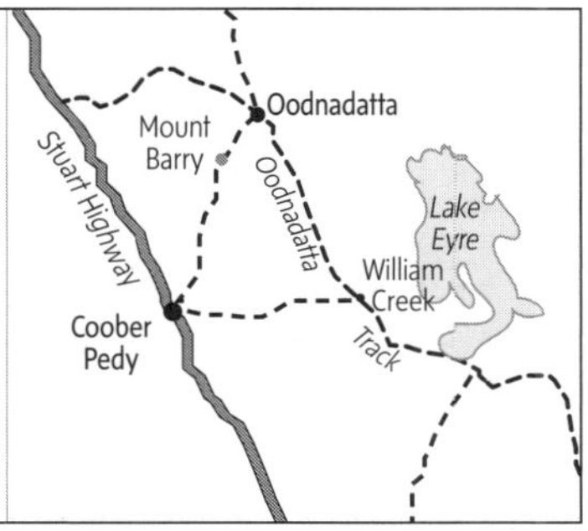

It has been **g** ______________ for the purpose of **h** ______________

a **i** ______________ that follows the Coober Pedy mail **j** ______________.

Like all travel advertising text it includes tour **k**______________,

accommodation **l**______________ and transport **m**______________

as well as examples of tourist **n**______________.

Fact File reproduced from Michael Gebicki's Desert Storm article in Sunday Life magazine.

2 The following colloquialisms occur in the passage 'The Oodnadatta Track'. Match them to their meanings:

a souvenired (a rail spike) ____

b skinny-dipping ____

c billed as (the largest cattle station on earth) ____

d cattle baron ____

i reputed to be

ii nude bathing

iii big cattle grazier

iv collected as a keepsake

3 Insert the colloqialisms from question 2 in the appropriate sentences below.

a Lang Hancock was a West Australian mining ______________.

b Some guests ______________ hotel towels, which becomes very expensive for hotel management.

c Circuses are often ______________ The Greatest Show on Earth.

d As the hole in the ozone layer widens ______________ is increasingly dangerous.

4 Convert to formal English.

a No worries, mate. I'll give you a hand. ______________

____

b I saw the bloke in the yellow wheels run the lights on Murphy Street.

____

5 Underline the correct alternative of these easily confused words.

a I was gratified/grateful for his help.

b A lung-fish can breath/breathe air.

c Alcohol will be prohibited/inhibited at the party.

d Frank was a social/sociable fellow with many friends.

e Freedom of speech is the base/basis of our argument.

Quick think

1 Using the prefix *trans~* (from the Latin word meaning *across*) complete the following.

a crossing a continent — transc _ _ _ _ n _ _ _ _ l

b to change totally — transf _ _ m

c to give blood to someone — transf _ _ e

d to break a law — transg _ _ ss

e to pierce with a spear — transf _ x

2 *Trans~* and light: insert the missing letters.

a can be seen through — trans _ _ _ _ _ t

b allows light to pass through — trans _ _ c _ _ t

3 *Trans~* and modern times: insert the missing letters.

- **a** containing genetic material from another species transg _ _ _ c
- **b** mid-flight airport stopover lounge trans _ t lounge
- **c** surgical organ replacement transp _ _ _ t
- **d** company with business worldwide transn _ t _ _ _ _ l

*P*roofreading

1 Correct spelling, vocabulary and usage.

Their were heaps of people at the Henley-on-Todd regatta. The dry river bed of the Todd felt hot alsorts of strange boats propeled by flying feet charge towards the finnish line. Crowds to rival the Americas Cup yatching crowds in enthusasm barraked for all manner of craft, from carboard boxes and cast iron bathtubs to flatened beer can hulls flying football jersee flags.

2 Correct any incorrect homonyms.

The tore bus carefully inched its way along the narrow rode that wound down the mountain. The few passengers awake did not here the driver mutter to himself that this was the last time he'd drive a heard of lazy tourists around who only slept or red their silly books and never once looked out the window. He piered hard through the dusty windscreen and thought longingly of the ready billabong in the valley below where he could swim while the passengers soughted themselves out.

Idiom

Explain:

1 Give us a break. The noise is too much! ________________________________

____

2 'That's rorting the system,' he declared angrily. ________________________________

____

Writing paragraphs and whole texts

1 Think about getting out of bed on a cold morning. Recall what you hear and see and feel and smell as you decide to get up. Make a list of these in the order you experience them. Beside them write as many phrases as possible that will describe exactly what that sound, smell or sensation was like.

e.g. *cold—made my eyes water—made my nose run—a cold wet dribble at the end of my nose*

____

____

____

____

____

2 Using your list about that cold morning write a plan, on your own paper, for four paragraphs describing the whole experience of getting up that day. Sort your list notes into groups of related experiences and put each group into a separate paragraph.

3 Write a topic sentence for each paragraph. Remember topic sentences introduce the new material that is in each paragraph, so they will all be different. Try to start each one in a different way, e.g. *When I … Then it was that I … Faced with that what could I … There was no alternative but to …*

4 Remembering that the point of a description is for you to make your reader feel and see and smell and think exactly what you do as you get out of bed on a cold morning, use your plan and your topic sentences to write:

a an introductory paragraph about getting up on that day

b a concluding paragraph about the same thing.

Chapter test

1 Circle the misspelt word.

a comemmorate **b** solitary **c** resourceful **d** bitumen

2 Which sentence is correct?

a This species of snake are venomous.

b This species of snake is venomous.

3 Which sentence is correct?

a May I go swimming this afternoon?

b Can I go swimming this afternoon?

4 Circle the correct alternative in this sentence.

I was gratified/grateful by the reception my speech received.

ANSWER SECTION

CHAPTER 1: SPEECH

Comprehension

1 Jagera
2 a
3 b
4 d
5 **a** in sport
b in the arts and intellectual activities
6 false
7 false
8 Bonner asked them to:
a end divisions between black and white;
b work together to solve problems

Writing skills

1 c
2 true
3 you
4 d
5 verbs
6 *on some occasions*
7 b, c
8 cooperation
9 us
10 b
11 **a** tick
b tick
c X
d tick

Focus on punctuation

1 **a** Rev. John Flynn
b The Rt Hon. Justice Tonelli
c Flt Lt Ellen Marcos
2 **a** Anzac Day April 25
b HMAS Melbourne
c Cathy Freeman
d Sydney Olympic Games
e E.K. Golding and Sons, Jewellers
f Emperor Napoleon of France invaded Russia.
3 **a** The cosmopolitan city of Sarajevo was tragically devastated during the Bosnian War.
b Uruguayans drink a thick tea called maté made from the leaves of the Ilex shrub.
c Paul Keating's speech known as the Redfern Park Statement was the first public admission that First Australians had suffered at the hands of European settlers.
4 The Australian arts scene has seen significant contributions by First Nations writers, singers, actors, poets, dancers and songwriters—David Gulpilil, Ernie Dingo, Maroochy Baramba, Jimmy Chi, Mudrooroo, Oodgeroo Noonuccal, Possum Tjapaltjari and Leah Purcell, not to mention the Bangarra Dance Theatre, to name a few.

Select a word

1 proclaim
2 eulogise
3 indict
4 appeal
5 orate
6 eulogise

Grammar

1 **a** Nova Peris-Kneebone was one of our Olympic athletes in the Nineties.
b The first Australian cricket internationals were an all-Aboriginal team.
c The Australian Women's Netball team is the reigning champion.
d Our high school plays touch football.
2 **a**–X, **b**–X, **c**–S, **d**–S
3 **a** is a dangerous pastime
b has become a popular activity
c see wonderful subterranean chambers
d find their pleasure in invisible worlds under the microscope
4 **a** The bushwalkers
b lightning
c gaily striped fish
d lizards
e Our friends

Word study

1 **a** church
b court
c university
d funeral
2 **a** a minister of religion
b a king or his herald
c a prosecutor
d a professor
3 **a** appeal
b homily
c lecture
d oration

4 **a** eulogy
b sermon
c dissertation
d appeal
e address

Evaluating other people's writing

1 *Whoever heard of a racist penguin?*
2 The fifth sentence (*Yet this sort of assertion…*)
3 humour
4 *doesn't it*
5 concrete, issue

Word usage

1 **a** hear
b there
c Where
d Whose
e They're
f here
g your
h Their
i Who's
2 **a** their
b there
c there
d whose, wear
e hear
f there
g your
h where
i who's, there

Quick think

1 **a** arboreal
b arboretum
c arbour
2 f
3 mahout
4 **a** plant, shrub, tree
b grasslands, scrub, forest
c scotch thistle
d bush

Proofreading

The eulogy for Fred Bates was delivered by his son, Charlie, whose success in Sydney as a criminal lawyer had always given him great pride. Fred was never short of words himself and had always told Charlie:

'Don't gobble like a turkey. Speak clearly. They have to hear you right down there at the back of the room.'

Charlie did his father proud at the funeral. He spoke so well people wept where they sat and did not hide their tears.

Idiom

1 Don't try to deceive me.
2 He had no energy to go any further.

Writing paragraphs and whole texts

1 Example answer
a Do the Simpsons have anything to answer for?
b Ladies and Gentlemen, The Simpsons have a lot to answer for.
c Since the Simpson family burst onto our screens, we have seen a virtual epidemic of Bart Simpson look-alikes selling everything from cheeseburgers to post office pens. Doh! That Simpson excuse for smart repartee has become part of our language.
d The Simpsons *do* have a lot to answer for.
3 **a**–iii, **b**–vi, **c**–iv, **d**–i or ii, **e**–v

Chapter test

1 true
2 appeal
3 Capt. James Cook
4 award

CHAPTER 2: SHORT STORY

Comprehension

1 c
2 a
3 c
4 The caver used a lamp, not a torch.
5 c
6 b
7 He thought the creatures making the noises had gone.
8 c

Writing skills

1 first, identification, subject
2 paragraph 4 and the lack of cave smell
3 blackness
4 metaphor—*a thousand little sand devils jabbing their tridents into my lungs*
5 giggled
6 c
7 *I closed my eyes*
8 c
9 c
10 c
11 b

Focus on punctuation

My mind went off at a tangent. I opened the drawer of my desk where I'd left Gustav's charm. I pulled it out, and tossed the bullet and its broken silver chain in front of Mr Dickson.

'Have you seen this, Mr ah-hmm Dickson?'

He slowly reached out to pick up the object. He held it close to his eyes, then gave a smile. I said, to prompt him, 'Russell told me this was Gustav's lucky charm. It's a parabellum bullet—out of a German machine gun.'

That extra information was superfluous. Mr Dickson smiled again.

'It may be Gustav's charm, but it's not a parabellum bullet.'

Select a word

1 fragile
2 brittle
3 feeble
4 frail
5 mobile
6 immobile
7 prudent
8 imprudent

Grammar

1 **a** compound **b** compound
c complex **d** complex

2 **a** Charlie will not bat
b The vet stroked the cat
c They were safe in the deep cave
d I will not climb onto the roof

3 **a** When the sandbar collapsed
b because those areas are not patrolled by lifesavers
c If you cannot see the bottom
d when the shark alarm sounded

4 **a** main
b dependent
c dependent
d main

Word study

1 **a** canvass
b compliment
c effect
d discreet
e canvas

2 **a**–iii, **b**–i, **c**–ii, **d**–v, **e**–vi, **f**–iv

3 **a** supercritical
b superfluous
c superhuman
d supermarket
e supersonic
f supernatural

Word usage

1 **a** legendary
b add
c approached
d inquired
e urgency
f birth
g condition
h shot

2 anecdote

3 **a** generous
b unique
c pretty or sky
d enamelled or pretty

4 Suggestions:
a disappointment
b an exceptional or most enjoyable
c best or finest

5 Suggestions:
a fashionable clothes
b silly or foolish
c stole my running shoes; reported them.

Quick think

1 **a** speleology
b speleologist
c shaft
d floor
e subterranean

2 **a** dank
b gloomy
c claustrophobic
d mystified
e petrified

Proofreading

Loud noise over extended periods can affect your hearing. Music channelled directly into the ear via earphones damages aural sensitivity. When naturally loud music is complemented by volume controls set on maximum, damage is certain and permanent.
Too many people do not realise that their hearing is a very delicate mechanism until it's too late. Most people do not know they're deaf until someone says 'Turn that radio down. I can't hear myself think.'

Idiom

1 We will present the plan/idea and ask people what they think of it.

2 He is a friend only when times are good and will disappear when you are in trouble.

Writing paragraphs and whole texts

2 d, f, b, e, g, c, a

Chapter test

1 true
2 discrete
3 and
4 colourful, striped, smart

CHAPTER 3: NEWSPAPER REPORT

Comprehension

1 May
2 Mrs Duel wrote her will on the side of a *Daily Telegraph* crossword puzzle.
3 c
4 The will made sense, it was properly signed and it carried the instruction to its finder not to throw it away.
5 c
6 She found the publication date of the puzzle.
7 false
8 unknown
9 If a later will were found, the puzzle will would be invalidated.

Writing skills

1 **a** crossword puzzle
b mystery
2 pun
3 b
4 true
5 b
6 b
7 The first part deals with the problem, the second with its solution.
8 scrawled
9 It is the title of the newspaper.

Focus on punctuation

1 **a** Henry's horse the mechanic's spanner
a praying mantis' wings/a praying mantis's wings
b the team's loss a lonely bird's cry
an audience's enthusiasm
2 **a** ships' cats, guitars' strings, girls' jeans
b men's hats, geese's yard, sheep's trough
3 **a** Abebe Bikila's
b Williams's/Williams'
c goose's
d Ben Lomas's/Lomas'

Select a word

1 adverse
2 averse
3 adapt
4 adhesion
5 excess
6 all ready

Grammar

1 **a** The flag S
b Sailors P
c The orchestra S
d Farmers and their dogs P
2 **a** have fallen ill
b is drawn
c are
d are required
3 **a** is
b disagree
c are

Word study

1 **a** adverse
b already
c excess
d adhesion
2 **a** access
b adopt
c all ready
d adherence
3 **a** X, adopt
b X, averse
c X, already
d X, access
e tick

Evaluating other people's writing

1 a
2 stranded
3 volunteers
4 b
5 repetition
6 b

Word usage

1 **a** nor **b** is
c is **d** or, was
2 **a** is **b** was
c is **d** was
3 **a** are **b** is
c was **d** is

Quick think

1–c, **2**–g, **3**–e, **4**–i, **5**–h, **6**–k, **7**–f, **8**–a, **9**–j, **10**–b, **11**–d

Proofreading

Pauline's friend was averse to visiting the zoo on an excursion. 'All those sorts of animals are on science videos already,' she complained.

After coffee at Antonia's she admitted she actually liked going to see the zoo's creatures but she hated the excess of walking you had to do there.

Idiom

1 I always keep ten dollars in case I need it unexpectedly.
2 She behaves as if she is superior to those around her.

Chapter test

1 false
2 **a** tick
b tick
c X
d tick
3 false
4 is

CHAPTER 4: ADVERTISEMENT

Comprehension

1 Pattaya beach
2 false
3 false
4 yes
5 phone, Internet, street address
6 false
7 false
8 b

Writing skills

1 b
2 sunshine, dramatically good price
3 **a** a palm-fringed beach and water
b the factual text from the inducement text
4 the reader
5 contrasts
6 persuade
7 second sentence
8 a
9 camping, trek or trekking
10 a, b, c, f
11 a
12 c
13 sell

Focus on punctuation

1 **a** Lt Col. Christopher Sparks has been appointed to Holsworthy base.
b Dr and Mrs Abramovitz will be attending the dinner hosted by Charles Coe, MLA.

2 **a** ?
b !
c .
d .
e ?
3 **a** X
b tick
c tick
d X
4 **a** Why is this work incomplete? Why, it's not even half-finished! Finish it immediately!
b To whom should I address this letter? Bob? His father? His mother? All of them together?
5 How will we know if it's Rev. Bill Smith, Dr Barry Howson or Corp. Charlie Groves if they're all out of uniform? Dashed if I know how we're supposed to know!

Select a word

1 **a** gamble
b bowl
c snuffle
d speck
2 flip, raise, lever, heave
3 possibility, feasibility, necessity

Grammar

1 **a** that/which
b whose
c who
2 **a** Jim Kalamiotis, whose grandfather had been a prawn fisher back in the Greek Islands, is just one of the third generation of his family to go trawling.
b Gareth Evans, who was a politician, also became known as a statesman in world affairs.
3 **a** As Nick practised his trumpet in the backyard, a yellow moon, which rose over the end of the street, smiled benignly.
b A slow tugboat chugged under the traffic-choked bridge that arched over the harbour.

Word study

1 **a** politician
b feasible
c necessary
d possible
2 air, water, food, shelter
3 **a** trek
b trudge
c shuffle
d stroll
e amble
4 **a** diplomat
b possible
c feasible
5 b, c, a, d

Word usage

1 **a** sites, click, browse
b subscribe, only $9.95 a month, free CD Starter Pack
2 **a**–iii, **b**–ii, **c**–ii, **d**–iii
3 **a** curious
b strategy
c budding

Quick think

1 **a** astronomy
b astronaut
c astrophysics
d astrologer
2 **a**–ii, **b**–i
3

remote	ii	with appliances
ride-on	iv	on grass
silly-mid-on	i	in a cricket game
knot	v	measuring speed at sea
tat	iii	in lace-making

Proofreading

1 **a** politician
b necessary
c feasible
d trudge
2 It was Dr Jonas Salk who invented the first polio vaccine. And who was Dr Salk? He was one of the twentieth century's great medical scientists, along with Drs Fleming and Florey whose work with penicillin gave the world antibiotics to fight bacterial disease.

Idiom

1 His argument was not supported by evidence, so it could not win.
2 This is a sarcastic comment to someone so glum she cannot say a pleasant thing to anyone.

Chapter test

1 The store that sells surf gear is having a sale.
2 no
3 no
4 !

CHAPTER 5: SCRIPT

Comprehension

1 false
2 Ralph, Jack
3 b
4 b
5 a
6 c
7 The election was conducted held under normal circumstances but it was free and democratic because there was more than one candidate, everyone voted and the candidate with the most votes was elected leader.

Writing skills

1 c, b, a
2 five (clearing, tropical island, those present, Ralph holds conch, blows conch three times.
3 voice production

4 audience
5 *Kids' names! Why should I be Jack? I'm Merridew.*
6 reaction, reaction
7 d
8 a, b
9 a, d
10 incidents, issues, incident, issue
11 The humour underlines the age of the small boys. It shows the gap between them and the older boys, who realise there are responsibilities to be faced that require leadership.

Focus on punctuation

1 **a** 'The centre light is not focused!' the director shouted.
b 'Where is my sword?' wailed the boy playing Hamlet.
c Macbeth famously asked, 'Is this a dagger which I see before me?'
d The fog machine put out so much fog that the actors were calling, 'Where are you? I can't see you!'

2 'Do you ever have nightmares?' Peter asked his brother.

'Not any more. I used to have them when I was little.'

'What sort of things did you dream about, David?' 'Oh, getting lost, falling down holes, that sort of thing. What are your nightmares about, Petey?'

'Getting thumped up by Skink.'

'Who's Skink? Is he that kid in Year 10 with the red hair?'

'Yeah, that's him.'

'Look, Petey, if he's bothering you, you tell me and I'll sort it out. No one's bullying my little brother.'

Select a word

1 argument, arguable
2 analysis, analytical
3 discussion, discursive
4 consideration, considerate

Grammar

1 **a** Our class (went) to see the Bell Shakespeare Company's production of *Hamlet*.
b To see a live production of any play (is) a thrilling experience.

2 **a** finite verb
b helping verb
c infinitive
d finite verb
e finite verb

3 **a** was
b was
c had
d will
e were
f are
g is
h am

4 **a** is known
b to play
c will produce
d was well received

5 **a** She needs to rewrite that letter correctly.
b To practise continually is the way to improve.
c She and I are going to the Easter Show.
d Michael is acting the part of King Lear.
e The play opened yesterday./The play is opening today.

Word study

1 **a** conflict
b issue
c incidents
d character
e characterisation

2 **a** discuss
b analyse
c consider
d assess
e argue

3 **a** analyse
b assess
c discuss
d consider
e argue

Evaluating other people's writing

1 b, c, d, e
2 **a ii** Sally's rudeness
b ii the argument about Sally's entry

Word usage

1 **a** can
b may, can
c may
d can
e May

2 **a** from
b from
c from
d from

3 **a** May we join you for coffee after the show?
b Luhrmann's *Romeo and Juliet* is different from Zeffirelli's.
c If the star is ill, we may see her understudy perform tonight.
d correct

Quick think

1 **a** false
b true
c lunatic

2 **a** telescope
b telemarketing
c telecast
d telepathy
e telekinesis

3 **a** geology
b geography
c geothermal

Proofreading

1 **a** audition
b incident
c issue
d rehearsal
e argue
f dialogue

2 'What did J.M. Barrie write?' asked a student.
'*Peter Pan*,' came the reply.
'I thought that was a film.'
'Yes, it was, but it was a stage play before it was made into a film. I have a copy of the script. You may read it, if you like.'

Idiom

1 Don't talk to him. He's not listening.
2 I don't understand.

Chapter test

1	c	**2**	b
3	b	**4**	c

CHAPTER 6: CARTOON

Comprehension

1 b
2 c
3 She is sewing.
4 c
5 c
6 a

Writing skills

1 illustration, text
2 **a** harsh reality
b whim
3 buzz
4 bottom
5 The machinist is making a garment of the same fabric as the society lady's dress. She might even have made that very dress.
6 dress, hairstyle, expression
7 by the stack of completed shirts beside her
8 moods
9 d
10 a
11 **A**–i, **B**–iii, **C**–ii

Focus on punctuation

1 **a** David, the identical twin of Duncan, equalled their elder brother's 100 m record.
b Mr Jones, who always wears red socks, is our maths teacher.
c The men of the Kokoda Trail swam rivers, climbed mountains, cut their way through jungle and halted the enemy advance.
d He stowed bread, cheese, dried fruit and water in his backpack.
e In this park dogs, skateboards and bicycles are prohibited.

2 **a** He was looking for his best friend, a black and tan kelpie dog.
b King parrots, large birds with tomato red and emerald plumage, are mountain birds.
c Joseph, an unusually talented musician, can play both the flute and the bassoon.
d The land east of the Blue Mountains, the land first settled by Europeans, was land belonging to the Eora, Tharawal and Dharrug peoples.

Select a word

1 photocopier
2 photogenic
3 photo finish
4 photophobia
5 photojournalism
6 photographer

Grammar

1 **a** Someone said you are <u>intending</u> to become a cartoonist.
b Kaz Cooke is <u>criticising</u> the harsh system of outsourcing clothing manufacture.
c Larson's most famous cartoons show cows who are <u>behaving</u> like people.
d starring
e dancing

2 **a** are gathering
b is frolicking
c are reliving
d are training
e are exhibiting

Word study

1 **a** caricature
b graphic
c illustration
d photograph

2 **a** meticulous
b bold
c linear
d illustration/depiction

3 **a** false
b true
c false
d true

4 **a** caricature
b illustration
c photograph
d bold

5 **a** graph
b phosphorus
c phoenix
e philosopher
f agoraphobia

Word usage

1 **a** Cartoon B
b Cathy Freeman
c i, ii, iv, vi
d comfort
e disapprove
f ii

2 **a** i The lofty high mountains reached into the clouds.
ii Floodwaters turned the plain into a gigantic enormous lake.
iii Duck Creek used to be a murky, discoloured, stinking, foul-smelling stream.
b i Old Mr Ho was a shipwright in Singapore.
ii Mrs Townsend is a counsellor.
iii Cliff Small is a referee.
c i renege
ii authorise
iii enrol
d The old Budgewoi fisherman fished on the river bank all day but went home empty-handed.

Quick think

1 **a** facial features
b gait
c mannerisms
d gestures
2 **a**–ii, **b**–iv, **c**–i, **d**–iii
3 **a** brief
b precise
c compact
d complement

Proofreading

'We all live in a yellow submarine,' sang my father, rather tunelessly I thought. My mother broke in with a snatch from 'Eleanor Rigby' about 'all the lonely people', but it was when my elder brother, whom I'd always thought sensible, began banging two tins together and bellowing 'Penny Lane' that I knew my family was seriously deranged. Old-fashioned Beatlemania had them in its grasp.

Idiom

1 He lives very near me.
2 He does not have a single valid argument to put.

Writing paragraphs and whole texts

1 **a** The original cartoon showed an enormous bug with a tiny human crawling on its back.
b The original cartoon showed a goldfish out of its bowl, singing and playing a fiddle.

Chapter test

1 no
2 auditory
3 That man, the one with the feather in his hat, does not look very well.
4 no

CHAPTER 7: POEM

Comprehension

1 b
2 Woolloomooloo, Domain, Kings Cross
3 red clothes, barefoot, umbrella, dog
4 true
5 c
6 It is not raining, but because the sky shows an approaching storm the boy goes out knowing he will be caught in the rain.
7 Don't go out. It's going to rain and you'll get wet.
8 The elements are the forces of nature: wind, rain, lightning and thunder.
9 b

Writing skills

1 figurative
2 dominance
3 *oblivious*
4 *follows him obediently*
5 *gaze, stare*
6 the first three lines
7 the last two lines
8 *caught up*
9 *slips, grown-ups*
10 elements, braves
11 c
12 a, c, e

Focus on punctuation

1 The hard men of eighties cinema are now all old men: Steve McQueen, Clint Eastwood, Sylvester Stallone and Arnold Schwarzenegger.
2 Skimming through the plays of Shakespeare she came across Lady Macbeth's famous line: 'All the perfumes of Arabia will not sweeten this little hand.'
3 The causes of the Eureka rebellion were varied: resentment of the gold licence fee, police brutality and the provocative conduct of the covernment.
4 The Valley of the Kings has revealed unbelievable treasures: mummies of ancient Pharaohs, gold caskets, gold death masks and gold funerary gifts.
5 One of John O'Brien's most quoted lines about drought and flood is: 'We'll all be rooned, said Hanrahan.'

Select a word

1 chime
2 toil
3 gritty
4 clammy

Grammar

1 Suggestions:
a collected
b eaten
c repaired
d read
2 **a** i had hurried
ii has eaten
iii have gone
iv were caught
v ridden
vi swum
vii drunk
viii bought
b i chased
ii danced
iii flown
iv caught

3 **a** lied
b laid
c lain
d hanged
e hung
f bought
g brought
h laid
4 **a** X
b tick
c tick
d X

Word study

1 **a** harsh
b flecked
c shimmering
d livid
2 **a** coarse
b doughy
c sinuous
d fluid
3 **a**–iii, **b**–iv, **c**–i, **d**–ii
4 **a** scene
b scimitar
c sceptre
d science

Word usage

1 **a**–vii, **b**–viii, **c**–ix, **d**–xi, **e**–xii, **f**–v, **g**–x, **h**–i, **i**–iii, **j**–vi, **k**–iv, **l**–iv
2 **a**–M, **b**–MM, **c**–MM, **d**–M
3 **a** Miss Adams was a breath of fresh air in our classroom and very welcome.
b Carlos was a big man with sharp eyes and the strength of a lion.

Quick think

a screech, squawk
b twitter
c squeal
d thunders
e clinks, jingles
f plops

Proofreading

1 doughy, pungent, livid, sinuous
2 Australian teenager, Andrew Perrin, single-handedly sailed his yacaht, Seaflight, around the world in 1997. He was still only seventeen when he rounded Cape Horn at the foot of South America where so many ships have come to grief in the past.
3 the owner had <u>ridden</u> up
he <u>brought</u> up the local mounted police
and <u>jumped</u> into the billabong
If he had <u>swum</u>
before the troopers <u>caught</u> him

Idiom

1 He will trick you if he has the slightest chance to do so.
2 It means to take a risk or a chance.

Chapter test

1 b
2 a
3 brought
4 swum

CHAPTER 8: EXPLANATION/INSTRUCTION

Comprehension

1 headstock
2 b
3 c
4 narrow their bars
5 d
6 **a** carry their elbows high
b maximum leverage on the bars
7 They narrow their handlebars so they can get through tight spaces more easily.
8 80 centimetres

Writing skills

1 Information about adjusting other components of the bike.
2 *prepare*
3 c
4 correct
5 jargon
6 motocross/supercross
7 a, c, d
8 a
9 b
10 you
11 b

Focus on punctuation

1 **a** custom-isation
b orches-tration
c mountain-eering
d admin-istratively
2 **a** For sale: little-used Range Rover
b a short-sighted man
c Carley ordered a hot-dog.
3 **a** —the little man in the three-cornered hat and his hand inside his jacket—
b —Julie! Will you turn the radio down!—
c —these are the stock-in-trade of slapstick comedians.

Select a word

1 obstruct
2 sufficient
3 terrain
4 various
5 various
6 sitting

Grammar

1 **a** As I crawled into bed the moon climbed over the window sill.
b As I fished off the jetty the torpedo shape of a grey nurse shark darkened the water.
2 **a** A policeman arrested and charged the vandal carving his initial into a park bench.

c As he stopped to sniff the telegraph pole I noticed my dog's collar tag was missing.
d Ben was really looking forward to the roast dinner made of the turkey that had been fattened for weeks.

Word study

1 **a** terrain
b sufficient
c leverage
d maximum
e obstruct

2 **a** hitting
b shouting
c sleeping
d clipping
e flipping
f keeping

3 **a** adjustment
b obstruction
c sufficiency
d variety

4 **a** minimum
b facilitate
c insufficient
d depth
e standing
f divergent

5 **a** inanimate
b imprudent
c inefficient
d implicit
e impatient
f incapable

Evaluating other people's writing

1 **a** No
b No
c No
d No
e No

2 pH level, seed, eyes, hill

Word usage

1 **a** many
b fewer
c fewer
d much
e many

2 **a** less
b few
c few, many
d much
e few

3 **a**–iii, **b**–iv, **c**–i, **d**–v, **e**–ii

Quick think

a many
b herd
c majority
d schools/shoals
f many

Proofreading

1 Various hand tools are available for student use. They must be used appropriately—are you listening, Kylie?—No chisel can be used for leverage and screwdrivers can't be used to obstruct the movement of any machinery. Now see if you can cut two parallel 1 cm-deep slits in your wood without chopping off any fingers.

2 **a** X
b X
c tick
d tick

Idiom

1 I would not like to share her experience at all.
2 I am not taking sides on that issue.

Writing paragraphs and whole texts

1 **a** companions
b reputable
c Provide
d mixture
e opportunity
f Handle
g frequently
h principle

Chapter test

1 b
2 longXstanding
3 a
4 carat

CHAPTER 9: EXPOSITION

Comprehension

1 c
2 three
3 c
4 People do not do the course voluntarily.
5 false
6 increased
7 d

Writing skills

1 three obvious conclusions
2 appalling
3 d
4 the results of the weekend police blitz testing for drink-drivers
5 He projects that percentage onto the total driving population and counts the results as a real number.
6 a
7 *Sobering statistics*
8 b
9 c
10 *So how do we stop it?*
11 a
12 b, d

Focus on punctuation

1 **a** they're
b we're
c he's
d I'm
e you're
f she's
2 **a** We're
b aren't
c would've
d hadn't
3 **a** haven't
b should've
c could've
d mightn't
e needn't
f you're
4 **a** its
b its
c it's
d It's, it's

Select a word

1 deterrent
2 mandatory
3 complacent
4 controversial
5 statistics
6 appalling

Grammar

1 **a** weeping
b aspiring
c smiling
d The distressed woman wrung her hands and wept.
e The vet attended Henry's injured horse.
2 **a** the clamour of her 40-decibel accompaniment drowned out the shrieking lead singer.
b A sea eagle seized a shrieking mutton-bird chick from its nest.
c A skateboarding youth saved a child from being run over by a truck in Johnston Street.
d The laughing children played beach cricket on the sand.
e On the beach dying penguins lay covered in oil from a spill at sea.
f The dealer passed out the shuffled cards to the players.
g The gathered shellfish were packed in ice.

Word study

1 **a** impaired
b controversial
c deterrent
d complacent
2 **a** appalling
b statistics
c favour
d deterrent
3 **a** Yes
b No
c No
d No
4 **a** impaired
b favour
c mandatory
d appalling

Evaluating other people's writing

1 a, b, c, d, e, f, g
2 **a** *There's hostels*
b Paragraph 2, sentence 1
c *We could go trout fishing too.*
d there, there
e *all out over the range*

Word usage

1 **a** again
b back
c As a rule
d around
e and safeguard
2 **a** May
b can
c may
d Can
3 **a**–ii, **b**–i, **c**–i, **d**–ii
4 **a** clarify
b explain
c elucidate

Quick think

1 **a** chronology
b cosmonaut
c geology
d anthropology
e chronometer
f cosmopolitan
2 Time: milestone, precedent, instant, nanosecond, millennium, sundial
Law: bench, precedent, sentence, scales, wig, acquittal, verdict, justice, remand
Measurement: milestone, tonne, scales, knot, pedometer, micron, furlong, litre
Husbandry: flock, sericulture, calving, aquaculture, apiarist, micron, swine, stables

Idiom

1 It is sealed so tightly no air can enter.
2 I do not value his opinion.

Proofreading

The fixing of P plates to the cars of newly licensed drivers is mandatory for the first year of driving. During that period a P-plated driver may consume no alcohol at all prior to or while driving. Neither can such a driver exceed 80 kilometres an hour.

'That's unfair,' many young drivers complain, citing the fact that many older drivers are anything but good drivers. However, statistics quite clearly prove that youth and excessive speed are a common and dangerous combination on our roads, almost as lethal as the combination of drinking and driving.

Chapter test
1 Panning for gold is a hands-on occupation.
2 b
3 A watching hawk dived on a field mouse in the grass.
4 We know where you're going.

CHAPTER 10: INTERVIEW

Comprehension
1 c
2 guitar
3 b
4 the Louisiana swamplands
5 the atmosphere
6 false
7 false
8 d
9 I don't keep trying to change or improve it.

Writing skills
1 d
2 third question
3 b, d
4 a
5 a
6 a, b, d
7 first question
8 a
9 b
10 a
11 b, c

Focus on punctuation
1 The book was in the library (and that surprised me since it is so popular) so I could finish reading it. (Note: dashes could replace brackets here.)
2 She always cooks with oil (not just any oil, mind you, but cholesterol-free canola oil) because she says it enhances the flavour of the dish. (Note: dashes could replace brackets here.)
3 Tweet! Tweet! Tweet! That budgie's driving me insane—put it outside.
4 The Southern Lights (scientists call them Aurora Australis) are a spectacular atmospheric display over the Antarctic. (Note: dashes could replace brackets here.)
5 Ring Ali—Write to Sarah—Return Kevin' book—Finish assignment.

Select a word
1 excavate
2 exhume
3 exhume
4 neolithic
5 biennial
6 neonate

Grammar
1 **a** against
b inside, in
c to
d on
e beside, in
2 **a** for/from
b towards, over
c around
d around, across
e out, at/over/across
3 **a** from
b with
c of
d of
e to
4 **a** from
b with
c to
d with
e to

Word study
1 **a** verbatim
b style
c technique
d research
e presentation
2 **a** verbatim
b style
c research
d technique
e presentation
3 **a** bisect
b neonate
c exhale
d quadrilateral
e exile
f bicycle
g quadrangle
4 **a** alligator
b imagine
c studio
d guitar
e character

Evaluating other people's writing
1 fourth question
2 b
3 a
4 a, b, c

Word usage
1 **a** many
b number
c fewer
d majority
2 **a** more/less
b majority
c amount
d many
3 **a** less
b few
c amount
d least
e minimum
f shortage

4 **a** clutch
b dozen
c couplet
d flotilla
e litres
5 nanosecond, microsecond, second, minute, hour

Quick think

1 **a** gig
b tour
c manager
d amplifier
e studio
f inspiration
2 **a** staccato
b presto
c crescendo
d tempo
e a cappella

Proofreading

Studio recording can be exhausting. Musicians, as well as the studio staff, need to understand the techniques of recording to ensure a good recording. Not many stars have their own studios as White has, and the majority of them have to rely on the skills of whatever studio they can persuade to like their style and sound. This probably sounds depressing—it's just show business.

Idiom

1 He was as valuable addition to the band.
2 They had no way of explaining their dog's escape.

Writing paragraphs and whole texts

1 b, c, h, i

Chapter test

1 b
2 tecnique
3 b
4 many

CHAPTER 11: MUSIC REVIEW

Comprehension

1 true
2 She has previously released a single cover song and this albu has confirmed that she is an artist of considerable talent.
3 false
4 The first two songs have the sound of an Olivia Newton-John singing style.
5 c
6 14
7 She sings ballads with a rural theme and she is described as *an Aussie country singer/songwriter*.
8 story
9 c

Writing skills

1 the title and subheadings
2 this is Felicity's first album
3 third
4 d
5 d
6 hit cover, tracks, charts
7 Olivia Newton-John is world famous. Connection with her style would enhance Felicity's musical reputation.
8 b
9 b
10 *could have as much appeal to contemporary charts as it will to country charts*
11 b

Focus on punctuation

1 **a** 'Please, may I have a go?' [No!' ['Why not?' ['Because I said so. that's why.'
b 'that's the best joke I've heard in a long time,' laughed Bob. 'Why don't you tell Mr George in Geography? It might even get us out of that test.'
c 'Move along now. There's nothing to be seen here,' said the policeman as he ushered the crowd away from the door.
2 **a** 'that's not my bag!' she shrieked.
b 'Why is that window opened?' his mother asked.
c 'Can't imagine where I left it,' muttered the voice in the dark.
3 'Do you want to go to the ABBA concert down at the hall tonight?'
'ABBA doesn't exist any more,' Amy told me bluntly.
'Yes, I know that, but this group sings all the ABBA songs and dresses like them too. Come on, it'll be a good night, I promise you.'
'Oh, all right, I suppose anything's better than watching reruns on TV,' said Amy with a smile.

Select a word

1 unintentional
2 potential
3 tribute
4 expectation
5 venture
6 tribute

Grammar

1 **a** of
b by
c of
d with
e from
2 **a** We met Leo and Paul at Circular Quay.
b Lauren promised to write to me as soon as she reached Bourke.
c the demonstration was held to protest against the ban on the wearing of earrings.
3 **a** to
b on
c within/beyond
d of
e on

Word study

1 **a** expectation
  b duet
  c scrutiny
  d version
2 **a** contemporary
  b potential
  c unintentional
3 a
4 b
5 **a** auction
  b auction
  c attempt
  d plans
  e pluck
  f pluck

Evaluating other people's writing

1 **a** Outstanding
  b inception
  c released
  d impact
  e broke
  f potential
2 b
3 a
4 a celebrity report

Word usage

1 a went to war
  b a Kenworth, not an Alfa Romeo Sports
2 **a** broke new ground
  b gave birth to, or was the beginning of, four new singles.
3 Elizabeth sowed the seeds of discontent among her neighbours. She watered them daily with visits to each woman, during which she remarked how strongly Mrs So-and-So felt and was rewarded finally with a harvest beyond her wildest expectations—a whole street demonstration outside the council chambers demanding Rose Street be closed to heavy trucks.

Quick think

1 amble
2 ambulance
3 labourers
4 ambulatory
5 portable
6 labour
7 portage
8 porter
9 laborious
10 laboratory

Proofreading

Because she was bored with watching football, Sally went outside, even though her mother reminded her it was very cold.

'I'm more tolerant of cold than you think, Mum,' she laughed. 'I'm not a potential flu victim. You and Dad have this expectation that I'll pick up a cold every time the temperature drops below 25 degrees.'

Idiom

1 He will not have the same attitude when he gets back.
2 *No show* means the person is absent.

Writing paragraphs and whole texts

1 d, e, c, a, b

Chapter test

1 no
2 b
3 **i** a comma
4 **b** a metaphor

CHAPTER 12: RADIO ADVERTISEMENT

Comprehension

1 c
2 b
3 United States of America
4 c
5 in the school holidays
6 c
7 The mind stores catchy tunes faster than fact, especially if the jingle is rhymed.

Writing skills

1 b
2 a free trip to L.A.
3 b, c, d
4 **a** i
  b *cruise*
5 a series of dots
6 It is the attention-getting anticlimax designed to make listeners laugh.
7 It separates the entertainment and information sections of the advertisement.
8 a, c, d, e, h
9 tone, sentence structure and vocabulary
10 It returns to colloquial language.
11 **c** If people want a free trip to Los Angeles they need this information on what to do to be eligible.

Focus on punctuation

1 **a** can't
  b wouldn't
  c won't
  d hasn't
  e haven't
  f aren't
2 **a** announcer's
  b sponsor's
  c disc jockey's
  d boys'
  e sailors'
  f mechanics'
  g cattle's horns
  h 1000 sheep fleeces
  i all fish's fins
3 **a** Commercial radio's extensive existence depends on the amount of advertising it can attract.
  b Triple J's success in recent years has been its ability to meet the youth market.

c 'We can't all be TV stars,' Michael's father told him.
d 'We'll be getting married in St Mark's, Darling Point,' the soap star told the press.
e 'We're happy little Vegemites' is Australia's most successful advertising jingle.
f Australian cricketers' baggy green caps are known all over the world.

Select a word

1 assert
2 broadcast
3 intone
4 advertise
5 visualise
6 produce

Grammar

1 **a** <u>His</u> uncle told <u>them</u> to surf between the flags.
b The band lost all <u>its</u> equipment in the accident.
c '<u>Your</u> guitar is not here!' yelled <u>his</u> friend.
d their, my
e Her, it

2 **a** She invited him and all his friends to a video-veg-out night.
b 'He's nicked me spikes,' he grumbled.
c She wanted to turn it off but couldn't find its 'off' switch.
d It was bright green and it said: 'Go back. Wrong way.'
e She chased a mouse into the kitchen where it ran under a fridge leaving her lying on her belly and whining as only a thwarted cat can.

3 **a** agencies
b dog
c Hari
d word
e director

4 **a** their
b her, it, her
c her, her
d their, they
e mine, my, it

Word study

1 **a** targeted
b broadcast
c commercial
d comparison
e assertion
f niche
g claim
h intonation
i rhetorical
j advertisement

2 **a** rhetorical
b targeted
c comparison
d commercial
e advertisement
f niche

3 **a** forehead
b posthumous
c midday
d antibiotics
e antidote
f precedent

4 **a**–iv, **b**–iii, **c**–everything except sculptures

5 c

Evaluating other people's writing

1 No
2 The buyer won't find the address because no house number is given.
3 Parental guinea pig colour is unnecessary information.
4 He doesn't identify which males and which females have these colours.
5 No price for male guinea pigs is given.
6 This is an ineffectual advertisement because the buyer does not know exactly what is offered for sale or how to contact the vendor.

Word usage

1 **a** bought
b inferring
c lay
d translucent
e flair

2 **a** inferred
b transparent
c translucent
d laid
e lay
f bought, brought
g flare
h flair

Quick think

1 **a** fait accompli
b in flagrante
c magnum opus
d ipso facto
e in extremis

2 **a**–iv, **b**–v, **c**–i, **d**–ii, **e**–iii

Proofreading

1 Radio advertisements, unlike television advertisements, rarely address children. This arm of the media aims commercials at teenagers and adults. The reason is simple. Children do not listen to radio until they are old enough to appreciate pop music.

2 Fatimah and Felicity planned <u>their</u> excursion to the zoo very carefully. They would catch the train to Circular Quay and then a ferry to Taronga. As it turned out they just missed one. It was hauling in <u>its</u> gangplanks as they reached the wharf. <u>They</u> decided to sit and watch the buskers playing <u>their</u> various instruments on the Quay until another ferry arrived.

Idiom

1 David is awkward and clumsy, and is out of place in the gym.
2 The excuse has been used before and is no longer believable.

Writing paragraphs and whole texts

1 c, d, f. The other alternatives would be unsuitable because they do not match the target market's interests.

Chapter test

1 targetted
2 its
3 The captain knew that his team's morale was crushed by their opponents' height and bulk.
4 lay

CHAPTER 13: MAGAZINE ARTICLE

Comprehension

1 a
2 c
3 d
4 Balloons, banners, invitations and plates all match in colour.
5 false
6 toddlers, 7- and 8-year-old boys
7 competition between parents

Writing skills

1 c, d
2 This is quoted as evidence of party change from experts, people in the party business.
3 quotes
4 She gives examples from both Sydney and Melbourne
5 describes, make/convey
6 d
7 b, e
8 b
9 authenticity
10 taunted
11 b, c
12 e

Focus on punctuation

1 **a** The refrain 'Who'll come a-waltzing Matilda with me' is widely recognised.
b I read Winton's 'Blue Boy' over Christmas.
c The way Elaine says 'Oh, my dear!' is most annoying.
d Nobody in Year 8 enjoyed Davison's 'Man-shy', but everyone thought Gleitzman's 'Two Weeks With the Queen' hilarious.
e Richard Lovelace's line: 'Stone walls do not a prison make' is a famous quotation.
f 'For the love of Mike! Put things away when you're finished with them!' roared his brother.

2 **a** 'The death of the tiger shark in Winton's "Blue Boy" was the saddest thing I have ever read,' Benni confided to his mate.
b 'Do you think I'd make a good clown—Hey there, kiddies, I'm Clarrie the clown—well, what do you think, Lisa?' Toby asked his sister.

Select a word

1 **a** humorous
b amusing
c hilarious
d uproarious

2 **a** pier
b assent
c meddle
d guerilla

Grammar

1 **a** 'Fingerlings' are fish the size of your little finger,' the Inspector of Fisheries scolded the poacher.
b The great success of Peter Jackson's Ring films was the combination of live film with animation.
c In early Sydney habitual criminals were sent to Norfolk Island.
d Henry Parkes introduced public education in New South Wales in 1870.
e Australia's Ian McDougall leads the world in ocean temperatures research.

2 **a** Addiction
b concern
c distress
d Education, aspiration
e terror, thought

3 **a** savagery
b weariness
c kindness
d ambition
e amiability
f value

4 **a** suspicion
b vengeance
c intention
d irritation
e acceleration
f belief

Word study

1 **a** vague
b lavish
c daunted
d affluent

2 **a** recall
b threaten
c obsessive
d coordinated

3 **a** recollection
b affluence
c obsession
d coordination
e threat
f taunt

4 **a** poverty
b meagre
c encourage
d certain
5 **a** lavish
b suburbia
c vague
d taunted

Word usage

1 **a** i unique
ii savagely
iii kneeling
iv relocated
v hierarchical
vi isolation
b i Culling operations in Kruger National Park, South Africa, have produced a unique problem.
ii The trouble-making elephants are all orphans relocated to other parks after Kruger culling operations.
c They have not had adult elephants to teach them how to behave properly.
d i did in, macabre
ii teenaged human beings
iii metaphorically
2 it could be said
Despite the fact that
However
On the other hand
3 **a** we're
b where
c where
d wear
e we're
4 **a** yore
b you're
c you're
d your
e your

Quick think

1 **a** slapstick
b black
c satire
d situation
2 **a**–iv, **b**–iii, **c**–i, **d**–ii

Proofreading

Not coming from affluent suburbia, Kenny spent much of his holidays down on the quay fishing. His fishing story tonight was hilarious.

'You're never going to believe this. I caught a seagull. It swooped in and swallowed a little bream I was just reeling in. Took me twenty minutes to get the hook and line out of the stupid bird. And now I'm wearing everything he ate since he got up this morning!'

Idiom

1 This is most unlikely to happen.
2 It means the object is so repulsive you would not go anywhere near it. (A bargepole is a very long pole used to propel a barge along a river.)

Writing paragraphs and whole texts

1 **a**–N, **b**–M, **c**–M, **d**–N, **e**–N, **f**–M

Chapter test

1 affluence
2 true
3 c
4 your

CHAPTER 14: CLASSIFIED ADVERTISEMENTS

Comprehension

1 true
2 would not
3 'The Albatross'
4 is not
5 a quarter share in the ownership of a racehorse
6 He must have been lost.
7 false
8 false
9 At the end of training your dog will obey all instructions taught or the training fees will be refunded.
10 vendor, purchaser

Writing skills

1 b
2 abbreviated, excellent condition
3 or near offer
4 c
5 Jeep Cherokee Sports 94
6 all work guarantedd or no fee
7 midweek discounts
8 cross
9 market
10 c

Focus on punctuation

1 'Boots: black, brown, suede, patent; all styles, all sizes.' This catalogue entry stood out among the odds and sods of the auction listing—Taylor's Annual Clearing Sale listing, actually. I turned to Gino Pirelli, our next-door neighbour:

'Fancy some old-style footwear?'

He guffawed. 'Me? I wear runners, mate, runners with Pirrelli tread on them.'

2 **a**–iv, **b**–i, **c**–ii, **d**–i

Select a word

1 guarantee
2 required
3 porcelain
4 guard
5 charter
6 discount

Grammar

1 **a** she
b I
c I
d we
e he

2 **a** were
b were
c were
d were
e were

3 **a** If you were I you'd have the same trouble with chemical equations.
b If it were he who had to decide we'll still be waiting for a decision tomorrow.
c If I were she I'd apply for that job.
d It was they who volunteered to help the disabled students.

Word study

1 **a** guarantee
b discount
c collectables
d charter

2 **a** relationship
b required
c porcelain
d available

3 **a** **i** licence
ii permitted
b alcohol

4 **a** licensed
b licensed
c licence
d licence
e licence

5 **a** guild
b guess
c guest
d guilt
e guile
f guinea
g guest
h guava
i guardian
j guerilla

Evaluating other people's writing

1 reg. man. gears
2 with, body, without, willing to pay
3 d
4 advertiser contact details
5 The buyer is not offering nearly enough for what he/she wants to buy.

Word usage

1 **a**–v, **b**–iv, **c**–ii, **d**–i, **e**–iii
2 **a**–ii, **b**–iv, **c**–i, **d**–iii
3 **a**–iv, **b**–vi, **c**–v, **d**–vii, **e**–viii, **f**–ix, **g**–iii, **h**–ii, **i**–i

Quick think

1 **a** upholstery
b speakers
c wheels
d hubs
e owner's
f new

2 **a**–iv, **b**–v, **c**–vi, **d**–i, **e**–ii, **f**–vii, **g**–iii

Proofreading

My Dad loves selling things through the classifieds. Every Wednesday he'll be on the phone ringing the latest ad through to the office of our local paper. The trouble is then he'll go out on Saturday mornings.

'Just got to duck out for a few minutes'—and off he'll go. He's no sooner out the door than the phone will start ringing.

'My Dad's not available just now. He'll be back here in half an hour.'

When he's not back by eleven that's when I usually start selling things for whatever the caller wants to pay.

When he gets back ('Caught talking to Fred Pearce') he's always satisfied with the deal I've done. He tells me I should be a salesman when I leave school but he worries that one day I'll give a guarantee on one of his sales and then he will regret going out on Saturdays.

Idiom

1 I bought a very, very good bargain today.
2 This house has all modern conveniences such as a dishwasher and air-conditioning.

Writing paragraphs and whole texts

1 Holden sedan EH. Fully restored, immaculate. Fully recondit'd motor/gearbox. Reg. July 2013 $3800 ono. 02 6543 7910 a.h.

Chapter test

1 b
2 If it were my choice, I'd go to see a film.
3 guaranteed
4 licences

CHAPTER 15: FACTUAL DESCRIPTION

Comprehension

1 b
2 false
3 false
4 c
5 It is used as a runway.
6 dirt/gravel
7 c
8 true
9 That is how it is advertised.
10 too bushed

Writing skills

1 journey
2 blow-up cushion
3 f

4 condense
5 alliteration and rhyme
6 emphasise, exaggeration
7 wide-eyed
8 *carved*
9 c
10 stop, think

Focus on punctuation

1 **a** Dr Rashid's surgery is adjacent to Harris's bakery.
b 'Where's the mail for Augathella station?' asked the stockman.
c Pool rules are: no running, no jumping, no bombing and definitely no ducking.
d Eddie likes watching ants, the big red sugar ants that live under the old wattle tree.
e 'Where did you put my sneakers, Susan ?'asked her sister.

2 **a** 'I can't find it!" whispered the boy beside him. 'It's on Smithy's desk. It's called *Calculus for Fun* but it's not funny.
b The chest was full of gems: diamonds, emeralds, rubies, sapphires, even opals.
c Harry Petrecevic, the carpenter, has done an exceptional job restoring Foley's Folly, that derelict shack made of beer bottles on the outskirts of Coober Pedy.
d I wonder why he chose that shirt.
e We don't know if it's going to rain today.
Note: Single or double inverted commas may be used.

3 **a** shouldn't
b won't
c didn't
d can't

4 **a** ex. cond
b incl.
c ono
d tba
e expd.
f reqd.

Select a word

1 encounter
2 abandoned
3 remote
4 resourceful
5 bitumen
6 solitary

Grammar

1 **a** snake, is
b is
c car, were
d have
e are
f is
g is
h Has

2 **a** <u>May</u> I go to the disco on Friday?
b These joggers are different from those.
c Neither John nor Julie <u>eats</u> meat.
d It was <u>he</u> who broke the window.
e I wondered <u>whether</u> to take my umbrella.
f Brent threw the javelin right over <u>there</u>.

3 **a** whom
b who
c whose
d who
e whose

4 I threw wheat to the turkeys that were gobbling furiously with hunger.

Word study

1 **a** is
b thinking
c resourceful
d isolated

2 **a** remember
b commemorate

3 **a** enthusiastically
b wearily
c wistfully
d uproariously

4 **a** solo
b solitary
c solely
d soloist

Word usage

1 **a** informative
b descriptive
c facts
d attempt
e describe
f imagination
g written
h advertising
i trip
j run
k price
l availability
m details
n attractions

2 **a**–iv, **b**–ii, **c**–i, **d**–iii

3 **a** baron
b souvenir
c billed as
d skinny-dipping

4 **a** Don't worry, I'll help you.
b I saw the man in the yellow car drive through the red lights on Murphy Street.

5 **a** grateful
b breathe
c prohibited
d sociable
e basis

Quick think

1 **a** transcontinental
b transform
c transfuse
d transgress
e transfix

2 **a** transparent
b translucent
3 **a** transgenic
b transit lounge
c transplant
d transnational

Proofreading

1 There were many people at the Henley-on-Todd Regatta. The dry river bed of the Todd felt hot. All sorts of strange boats propelled by flying feet charged towards the finish line. Crowds to rival the America's Cup yachting crowds in enthusiasm barracked for all manner of craft, from cardboard boxes and cast-iron bathtubs to flattened beer-can hulls flying football-jersey flags.

2 The <u>tour</u> bus carefully inched its way along the narrow <u>road</u> that wound down the mountain. The few passengers awake did not <u>hear</u> the driver mutter to himself that this was the last time he'd drive a <u>herd</u> of lazy tourists around who only slept or <u>read</u> their silly books and never once looked out the window. He <u>peered</u> hard through the dusty windscreen and thought longingly of the <u>ready</u> billabong in the valley below where he could swim while the passengers <u>sorted</u> themselves out.

Idiom

1 Stop the noise. It is disturbing me.
2 It means cheating by manipulating the rules of any process or operation.

Chapter test

1 **a** comemmorate
2 b
3 a
4 gratified

Acknowledgements

The author and publisher would like to thank the following copyright holders for their permission to reprint.

Page 2, speech by Neville Bonner to the Constitutional Convention 1998 reprinted by permission of Wendy Southern; p. 5, extract from winning speech at the 1998 NSW Junior Multicultural Perspectives Competition reprinted by permission of Penelope Baker; p. 8, short story titled 'Bones', and p. 26, extract from a drama script titled 'The sound of the shell' reprinted by permission of Angeline Baker; p. 11, extract from *Too Old for Murder* reprinted by permission of Kevin Baker; p. 32, cartoon of society lady and machinist reprinted by permission of Kaz Cooke; p. 32, cartoon of three men with computers reprinted by permission of Patrick Cooke; p. 32, cartoon titled 'Underside' reprinted by permission of Phil Somerville; p. 35, cartoon about Olympics with person leaving the stadium reprinted by permission of Ron Tandberg/*The Age*; p. 35, cartoon of people watching the Olympics reprinted by permission of Cathy Wilcox; p. 37, two cartoons under the name Saviza reprinted by permission of Alan Irwin; p. 38 poem titled 'Storm over Woolloomooloo' by Peter Skrzynecki reprinted by permission of HarperCollins Publishers; p. 44, extract titled 'Smart set-ups' from *Dirt Bike: Tips and Techniques*, a Dirt Action Publication reprinted by permission of Martin White, Publisher; p. 56, article titled 'An interview with Tony Joe White' recorded by Greg Phillips for *Australian Musician*; p. 62, music review titled 'Nothing to hide' reprinted by permission of Bob Anthony and *Country Update* magazine; p. 65, article titled 'Hitmaker of the Decade' based on information provided by Country Music Radio Network reprinted by permission of Bob Anthony and *Country Update* magazine; p. 74, article titled 'Send in the Clowns' reprinted by permission of Jane Cadzow, *Good Weekend*, the *Sydney Morning Herald*; p. 86, extract from article titled 'Desert Storm' by Michael Gebicki in *Sunday Life* magazine reprinted by permission of Michael Gebicki; articles titled 'Crossword puzzle solves puzzle of old lady's will' on p. 14, 'Floods havoc' on p. 17, and article on drink-driving on p. 50 from the *Daily Telegraph* reprinted by permission of Kristen Pearson, Group News Services and Syndications Editor, News Ltd.

Efforts have been made to gain permission for all copyright material reproduced in this book, but we have not been successful in contacting all copyright holders. If you are one of these people, please contact Pascal Press.

NOTES

NOTES

NOTES